TAKEAWAYS

100 classics to cook at home

Edited by Robbie Davison and Fiona Shaw
Recipes by Tony Evans and Richard Simon

Can Cook Kitchen: Takeaways
Recipes by Tony Evans and Richard Simon
Edited by Robbie Davison
Photography by Alexandra Wolkowicz
Graphic design by Mike's Studio
Editorial consultant: Fiona Shaw
Proofreading by Judy Tasker
Indexing by Helen Vaughan
Printed and bound in Spain by Graficas

ISBN: 978-0-9564649-0-3

First published in April 2010 by
Can Cook Books, Conleach Road,
Liverpool L24 0TW.

www.cancook.co.uk
robbie@cancook.co.uk

CONTENTS

INTRO

Preparing takeaways at home: a guide

If you switch the television on or visit a bookshop the celebrity chef is everywhere, full of advice and tips – yet, for some reason, the messages aren't sticking. The evidence suggests that our eating habits are dominated by convenience shopping and takeaway meals and fewer families are choosing to cook at home – so we decided to combine takeaway food with cooking at home.

The world of the takeaway is either loved or loathed. Loved for its ability to provide a quick, tasty food fix. Loathed because of its reputation for serving up fatty, salty, unhealthy dishes.

This book deals with our love for takeaway meals – meals that when prepared with a bit of TLC, are less fatty, less salty, incredibly tasty and very easy to make.

We've tried to mirror the takeaway habits of the nation – Indian and Chinese food are the most popular, so we've recreated lots of dishes. The American theme is also strong, as well as our own English selection – then it's a trip around the world, allowing us to create those dishes we know to be favourites and some we believe should be.

We want you to use this book to create the takeaway experience at home – cooking for the whole family, cooking for friends, cooking just for you. We want you to experiment with new dishes, spices and all kinds of ingredients, but most of all we want you to improve your cookery skills and enjoy cooking.

Let's be honest, cooking a truly healthy takeaway type dish is difficult, particularly if you want it to taste good. Takeaways often contain meat, added salt, are cooked in oil, and in the case of some Indian and Thai dishes, can have some added cream or coconut milk. This method is often where the taste comes from and you need a bit of it to make cookery worthwhile – after all who likes to eat bland food? We certainly don't. The 100 recipes in this book tread the line between making sure every one tastes great and is as healthy as we can make it. Although we have to hold our hands up when suggesting dishes like the ribs on page 11 or the quarter pounder on page 16 – ribs contain their own fat and quarter pounders are exactly that, so are they ever going to be truly healthy? Probably not – therefore our advice is to go easy and share the portions.

In creating the recipes, we have thought hard about portion size. A takeaway bought from a local outlet is often measured by how big it is – it seems that bigger is better. But this is where some of the problems start, because big portions contain more fat, more salt and come packed with calories. We want to steer you away from this and into creating your own dishes that will still fill you up and leave you safe in the knowledge that you know exactly what has gone into your meal and that the ingredients are as fresh as you can make them.

The cost of each meal has also been a concern of ours, so each recipe contains the likely cost to you should you make it – let's face it if it's not value for money why would you try it?

We know in asking you to prepare your own takeaway meals, we are competing with the convenience of your local chippy, Chinese, balti house, kebab shop or even the ready meal – and convenience is a powerful thing. So we have tried to make the recipes as easy as we can, some like making pizza are slightly more complex, but mostly they will only take you 20 minutes max to bring them together, which is about the time it will take you to visit and buy from the local, wait for a home delivery or cook that ready meal.

There are enough recipes in here to tempt you into cooking healthier for yourself, or even creating a few dishes at a time for a meal for family, friends or both.

Let us know how you get on robbie@cancook.co.uk

A Can Cook first – this is the ultimate takeaway alternative, so let's set the tone for the whole book. Two tins + 20 minutes = tasty chicken curry with pilau rice, and not a drop of oil in sight. Easier than walking to the chippy...

TONY'S TWO TIN, NO FUSS, CURRY DINNER

THE CURRY

SERVES 2
COSTS £2

Each portion contains		
CALS 226	**FAT** 12g	**SALT** 1.7g
12%	16%	29%

of an adults' guideline daily amount

INGREDIENTS
50g leeks, sliced 1cm thick
50g carrot, peeled and diced to 1cm
50g potatoes, peeled and diced to 1cm
200g chicken thighs, chopped to about 2cm thick
1 tsp grated fresh ginger
1 small clove garlic, crushed
1 birds eye chilli, chopped
¼ tsp chilli powder
½ tsp ground coriander
½ tsp ground cumin
½ tsp ground turmeric
150ml half fat coconut milk
75ml passata
2 tbls fresh coriander, chopped
¼ tsp salt

EQUIPMENT
Sharp knife, grater, measuring jug, an aluminium takeaway container about 100 x 180mm (available from most supermarkets)

1. Put the leek, carrot, potato and chicken in the takeaway container.

2. Put the coconut milk, passata, ginger, garlic, birds eye chilli, chilli powder, ground coriander, ground cumin, turmeric, fresh coriander and salt in a measuring jug and mix well to combine.

3. Add the wet mix to the takeaway container and carefully mix, then place the lid on top and seal.

4. Bake in a pre-heated oven gas mark 6 / 200°C for 20 minutes, then remove and serve with pilau rice and naan bread (see page 66).

1. Put all the ingredients into 2 takeaway tins

THE PILAU RICE

SERVES 2
COSTS 70P

INGREDIENTS
225g basmati rice
2 spring onions, chopped
3 cardamom pods, crushed
½ tsp fennel seeds
½ cumin seeds
1 cinnamon stick
¼ tsp ground turmeric
300ml hot water
½ tsp salt
peeled rind from ¼ of a lemon
6 fresh curry leaves if available

Each portion contains

CALS	FAT	SALT
414	2g	1.3g
21%	2%	22%

of an adults' guideline daily amount

EQUIPMENT
Sharp knife, measuring jug, an aluminium takeaway container about 100 x 180mm

1. Put all of the ingredients into the takeaway container and carefully mix, then place the lid onto the container and seal it.

2. Place the container into a pre-heated oven gas mark 6 / 200°C for 20 minutes.

3. Remove from the oven, take the lid off and fluff up the rice with a fork, then serve with the chicken and vegetable curry in a box, or another curry of your choice.

3. Serve and enjoy!

It's said there's no such thing as American food. The food we tend to think of as American is – like the country – a melting pot of the flavours and tastes brought by its settlers and immigrants, adopted and adapted to the recipes you see today.

What is clear is that America can claim to be the takeaway capital of the world. Land of plenty, land of the burger – capturing the frontier spirit of those endless plains, meat is everywhere; food is fuel.

BBQ BABY BACK RIBS

DIY sticky pork ribs (with an added kick)

SERVES 2
COSTS £3

INGREDIENTS
500g spare ribs
2 tbls BBQ sauce (page 123)
½ star anise
1 tsp corn flour mixed with 2 tsp water

EQUIPMENT
Large pan with lid, small pan, small cup or ramekin, small casserole dish, sharp knife

1. Heat a large pan with about three inches of water, then place a small cup in it and a small casserole dish on the cup.

2. Put the ribs in a mixing bowl and add the BBQ sauce and star anise and mix well. Now place the ribs and all of the marinade in the casserole dish in the pan and put the lid on the pan.

3. Steam the ribs for about 1 hour and 15 minutes, then remove from the pan and drain the liquid into a small saucepan. Heat the liquid and whisk in the cornflower mixture, then continue to cook until thick. Add the ribs to the pan and coat in the sauce and serve.

Each portion contains		
CALS 437	**FAT** 28g	**SALT** 1.8g
23%	38%	30%
of an adults' guideline daily amount		

CHICKEN GOUJONS

SERVES 4
COSTS £3.50

INGREDIENTS
2 chicken breasts
2 tbls plain flour
small bunch coriander, chopped
1 tbls Cajun seasoning
2 cloves garlic, crushed
100g stale bread
2 eggs
salt and pepper
olive oil for frying

EQUIPMENT
Sharp knife, tongs, food processor, 3 mixing bowls, frying pan

1. Slice the chicken into small bite size strips and season with a little salt and pepper.

2. Place the flour into a bowl and season. Beat the egg in another bowl. Put the bread, garlic, Cajun seasoning and parsley in a food processor and blitz into breadcrumbs, then tip into the third bowl.

3. Take the chicken and coat in the flour and dust off any excess, then dip into the egg, making sure that the whole thing is covered. Finally coat in the breadcrumbs again, making sure the whole thing is covered.

4. Heat a frying pan with a little olive oil and fry the chicken in batches over a medium heat, for about 2 – 3 minutes on each side, adding a little more oil if needed.

5. Serve as part of a starter or with a salad as a main.

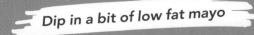

Dip in a bit of low fat mayo

SWEETCORN CHOWDER

Chow down on this one

SERVES 2
COSTS £2

INGREDIENTS
2 leeks, finely sliced
2 tbls olive oil
1 clove garlic, crushed
1 large baking potato, peeled and diced
350ml vegetable stock
400ml milk
300g can of sweetcorn, drained
salt and pepper to taste

EQUIPMENT
Sharp knife, large pan, measuring jug

1. Heat the oil in a large pan and fry the leeks over a medium heat for about 5 minutes to soften, then add the garlic and potatoes and continue to cook for 1 more minute.

2. Add the stock, sweetcorn and milk and bring to the boil, then simmer for about 10 – 15 minutes until the potato is soft.

3. Season to taste with salt and pepper and serve in bowls.

All hail this quick 'n' simple dish!

CAESAR SALAD

SERVES 2
COSTS £2

INGREDIENTS
½ clove garlic, crushed
6 anchovy fillets
1 egg yolk
½ tsp Dijon mustard
1 tbls lemon juice
100ml olive oil
2 tbls grated parmesan
1 large cos lettuce
150g ciabatta
1 tbls olive oil
4 slices streaky bacon
parmesan shavings
freshly ground black pepper

1. Place the garlic, 2 anchovy fillets, egg yolk, mustard and lemon juice in a food processor and blitz into a smooth paste, then with the processor still on, drizzle 100ml of olive oil in until smooth and creamy. Stir in the grated parmesan and season with black pepper.

2. Slice the ciabatta into 2cm cubes, drizzle with 1 tbls of olive oil and bake in a hot oven gas mark 7 / 220°C until golden. Meanwhile, grill the bacon on both sides until crisp and set aside.

3. Tear the cos lettuce into large pieces and place in a bowl along with the croutons, and drizzle most of the dressing over. Mix well and place in a large serving bowl. Put the remaining anchovy fillets and the crisp bacon on top, drizzle a little more dressing over and scatter the parmesan shavings on top.

CHICKEN BURGER

SERVES 2
COSTS £1.60

INGREDIENTS
1 chicken breast
1 tbls olive oil
1 clove garlic, crushed
1 tbls fresh thyme, chopped
zest from 1 lemon
2 buns of your choice
salt and pepper

EQUIPMENT
Rolling pin or something heavy if you don't have one, sharp knife, baking tray

1. Slice the chicken in half lengthways across the fillet so you have 2 flat fillets, then lay each piece between 2 layers of cling film and bash them with a rolling pin carefully until they are a little thinner (be careful when bashing not to rip the meat).

2. Place the chicken in a bowl and add the garlic, thyme, lemon zest and olive oil and mix well, leave to marinate for at least 30 minutes.

3. Heat the grill to high, then place the chicken breasts on a baking tray, season with salt and pepper and grill for about 3 minutes on each side or until cooked through.

4. Serve the chicken inside the buns with salad and sauce of your choice.

For a variation, take out the lemon and thyme and add 1 tsp ground cumin and 1 tbls fresh chopped coriander or 1 chopped fresh chilli, zest from 1 lime and 1 tsp smoked paprika. The combinations can be played with, so play...

Full of flavour, full of colour and healthier. Nothing like that fowl deep fried stuff.

CAJUN WEDGES

Chunky funky wedges – lighter than chips and ever so slightly spicy

SERVES 2
COSTS £1

INGREDIENTS
2 large baking potatoes
4 tbls olive oil
1 tsp Cajun seasoning
salt and pepper

EQUIPMENT
Baking tray, sharp knife

1. Preheat the oven to gas mark 6 / 200°C.

2. Now cut the potatoes into wedges about 2cm thick and place on a baking tray.

3. Drizzle over the olive oil and add the Cajun seasoning, then season with salt and pepper and mix well. Bake in the oven for 15 – 20 minutes, turning a couple of times, or until golden on the outside and soft in the middle (the time will depend on the thickness of the potato and the type).

4. To serve, drain onto kitchen paper and serve straight away.

MINTY LAMB BURGER

SERVES 4
COSTS £3.50

INGREDIENTS
1 red onion, finely sliced
1 tbls olive oil
450g lamb mince
3 tbls mint, chopped
salt and pepper to season
1 egg yolk

EQUIPMENT
Sharp knife, chopping board, frying pan, baking tray,
mixing bowl, wooden spoon, fish slice

1. Combine the mince, mint, egg yolk and salt and pepper
and blend until the mixture comes together. Divide into 4
equally-sized balls, and shape into burgers on a chopping
board. Cover and leave to chill for at least 30 minutes.

2. Lightly brush the burgers with the remaining oil, then
place them under the grill on a medium heat for 3 – 4
minutes on each side or until cooked to personal
preference. Serve.

*One to grab with both hands
and dive into. A big chunky bite.*

CLASSIC BURGER

SERVES 4
COSTS £3.50

INGREDIENTS
500g minced beef
100g medium onion, peeled and finely chopped
2 small cloves garlic, crushed
1 tbls dried mixed herbs
salt and pepper
4 slices of cheese
4 buns of your choice

EQUIPMENT
Sharp knife, fish slice, mixing bowl, baking tray,
frying pan

1. Preheat the oven to gas mark 6 / 200°C.

2. Put the onions, garlic and mixed herbs into a food
processor and blend.

3. Put the minced beef in a bowl along with the onion
mixture and season with salt and pepper. Mix well using
your hands – scrunch the mixture so everything is
well combined.

4. Shape the mixture into burgers and put them on a
plate. Refrigerate for about ten minutes to firm up a little.

5. Heat a non stick frying pan and fry the burgers for
about two minutes on each side, then transfer to a baking
tray and cook in the oven for five to eight minutes
depending on the size.

6. To serve, put the burgers in buns of your choice.

The ultimate iconic American burger

Each portion contains

CALS	FAT	SALT
551	24g	3.2g
29%	32%	53%

of an adults' guideline daily amount

Lambasted by some, loved by us, British food is hearty, wholesome and comforting. Based on simple, unfussy staples – English or Scottish beef, Welsh lamb, seasonal vegetables and regional cheeses – and using quality local ingredients, British cooking tends to use simple sauces to accentuate its flavours. You'll also see local dishes across the country – try our Lancashire hot pot or Cornish pasty.

BRIT

SHEPHERD'S PIE

SERVES 4
COSTS £4.50

INGREDIENTS
500g lamb mince
3 sticks celery, chopped
½ large onion, chopped
1 clove garlic, chopped
3 carrots, peeled and chopped
2 tsp plain flour
400ml brown chicken stock (see page 122) or a stock cube
4 tbls sunflower oil
4 large potatoes

EQUIPMENT
Sharp knife, chopping board, frying pan, saucepan, peeler, wooden spoon, sieve, potato masher, casserole dish

1. Heat 2 tbls oil in pan and brown the mince, then drain the excess fat.

2. Put 2 tbls of oil in a saucepan, add the celery, onion and garlic and cook on a medium heat until soft but not coloured. Then add the mince and flour. Cook for 2 minutes. Lower the heat, then add the stock and cook for 30 minutes.

3. Peel and dice the potatoes, place in a pan and cover with water. Bring to the boil and simmer until cooked. Drain and mash.

4. Put the cooked mince in casserole dish and top with the mashed potato. Place in a pre-heated oven at gas mark 4 / 180°C and cook until golden brown.

> **Not one you'd normally see in your local takeaway but great British food. We think it deserves to be everywhere.**

SCOTCH BROTH

SERVES 6
COSTS £6.50

INGREDIENTS
450g neck of lamb or mutton, excess fat trimmed
2.2 litres water
1 tsp salt
50g pearl barley
50g dried peas, soaked overnight and drained
1 large onion, peeled and diced
1 leek sliced
3 carrots, peeled and diced
1 small turnip, peeled and diced
¼ small white cabbage, shredded
2 sprigs of thyme

EQUIPMENT
Large saucepan, measuring jug, wooden spoon, sharp knife

1. Place the meat in a large pan with the water, barley and peas. Bring slowly to the boil, skimming off any foam as it appears.

2. Add the onions, leek, turnip and thyme and simmer very gently for about 2 hours until the meat is tender; add the cabbage for the last 15 minutes.

3. After 2 hours, remove the meat and shred, then return the meat to the pan and discard any fat or bones.

4. Season to taste with salt and pepper and serve with crusty bread.

> **Those winter nights just got warmer – one for a dip with crusty bread**

SMOKED HADDOCK FISHCAKES

SERVES 2 – 4
COSTS £3.50

INGREDIENTS
350g floury potatoes, eg Maris Piper or King Edwards, peeled and diced
200g smoked haddock fillet
300ml milk
2 tbls plain flour, seasoned
1 egg, beaten
8 – 10 tbls breadcrumbs
sunflower oil for frying
3 tbls fresh parsley, chopped
1 lemon
salt and pepper

EQUIPMENT
Sharp knife, chopping board, frying pan, saucepan, baking tray, peeler, mixing bowl, wooden spoon, whisk, sieve, potato masher

1. Preheat the oven to gas mark 7 / 220°C. Cook the diced potatoes in a large pan of boiling water for 12 – 15 minutes, until tender.

2. Place the haddock in a pan and pour the milk over it. Cover, bring to the boil and then remove from the heat and set aside for 5 minutes or so, until cooked through.

3. Drain the diced potatoes and return to the pan. Add some salt and pepper and mash the potatoes. Remove the fish from the pan and drain well, discarding the milk. Flake the fish into the potatoes and add the parsley. Shape the mixture into two or four firm even-sized cakes.

4. Dust the cakes lightly with seasoned flour. Put the beaten egg in a shallow bowl and spread out the breadcrumbs on a plate. Dip the fishcakes into the beaten egg and then into the breadcrumbs.

5. Heat sunflower oil in a frying pan and cook for 2 minutes on each side until crisp and golden; place in the oven on a baking tray at gas mark 4 / 180°C for 15 – 20 minutes.

6. Cut lemon into wedges and serve with fishcakes.

Smokey and tender flakes of fish – in a cake

CORNISH PASTY

MAKES 2
COSTS £3

INGREDIENTS
For the pastry:
250g plain flour
½ tsp bicarbonate of soda
½ tsp ground turmeric
3 tbls olive oil
100ml water

For the filling:
125 carrot, peeled and diced about 1cm
125g swede, peeled and diced about 1cm
200g potato, peeled and diced about 1cm
2 tsp fresh thyme, chopped
2 tsp fresh rosemary, chopped
50g frozen peas
1 egg white, lightly beaten
150g lean beef mince

Each portion contains		
CALS 415	**FAT** 14g	**SALT** 1.5g
21%	19%	25%
of an adults' guideline daily amount		

EQUIPMENT
Rolling pin, 2 mixing bowls, wooden spoon, sharp knife, measuring jug, pastry brush, salt and pepper

1. *For the pastry:*
Put the flour in a bowl along with the bicarbonate of soda, turmeric and olive oil. Slowly pour in the water a little at a time until a dough starts to form. Tip the dough onto a work top and gently knead a couple of times, then wrap in some cling film and set aside for about ten minutes to rest the dough.

2. *For the filling:*
Combine all the ingredients for the filling in another bowl and mix well, then season with a little salt and pepper.

3. When the pastry has rested – it should be a little softer – unwrap it and lightly flour a worktop. Roll the pastry out with a rolling pin until it's about 2 mm thick and cut into four circles; divide the filling between the centre of the circles and brush around the edges with the beaten egg white. Now fold over the pastry to make a pasty shape. and squeeze the edges to seal.

4. Place the pasties on a baking tray line with greaseproof paper and bake in a preheated oven gas mark 4 / 180°C for about 45 minutes.

Legend has it Cornish Miners would grasp their meaty snack, throwing away the dirty crust. Give it a whirl...

ISH, CHIPS ND MUSHY PEAS

SERVES 2
COSTS £2

INGREDIENTS
2 white fish fillets
2 large potatoes, cut into wedges
4 tbls sunflower oil
salt and pepper
2 tbls flour
2 eggs, beaten
200g bread crumbs
150g peas
1 clove of garlic, chopped
1 onion, chopped
a splash of water

Each portion contains		
CALS 608	**FAT** 18g	**SALT** 1.8g
31%	24%	30%

of an adults' guideline daily amount

EQUIPMENT
Sharp knife, chopping board, saucepan, baking tray, mixing bowl, wooden spoon, whisk, potato masher, fish slice, scales

1. Toss the potato wedges in 2 tbls oil and place on a tray. Cook in a pre-heated oven on gas mark 4 / 180°C for 30 minutes.

2. Coat the fish in flour and dip it in the egg before covering in breadcrumbs. Cook in a pre-heated oven at gas mark 4 / 180°C for 15 minutes.

3. To make the mushy peas, heat 1 tbls of oil and fry the onion and garlic. Add the peas with a splash of water, cook for 5 minutes until soft, then mash with a potato masher.

English classic – and celebrating its 150th birthday this year – delicious with peas. Newspaper optional!

STEAK AND ALE PIE

Don't forget the mash – this juicy pie creates the perfect gravy.

SERVES 4
COSTS £6

INGREDIENTS
900g braising steak, cubed
3 tbls sunflower oil
1 medium onion, peeled and sliced
1 tbls plain flour
1 tbls Worcester sauce
2 sprigs of thyme
1 tsp English mustard
1 bay leaf
150ml beef stock
125ml ale
225g mushrooms, sliced
450g puff pastry

EQUIPMENT
Sharp knife, wooden spoon, large pan, rolling pin, oven-proof dish

1. Heat the oil in a large pan and cook the onions over a medium heat for about 5 minutes until soft. Add the beef and fry until browned. Stir in the flour and cook for 1 minute, then add the Worcester sauce, thyme, mustard, bay leaf, beef stock, mushrooms and ale.

2. Bring slowly to the boil and simmer with the lid on for about 1½ hours until the meat is very tender.

3. Season to taste with salt and pepper and transfer to an oven-proof dish. Roll out the puff pastry to the thickness of a pound coin – place over the top and trim the edges.

4. Bake in a pre-heated oven at gas mark 6 / 200°C for 20 – 25 minutes until pastry is golden and serve with mashed potatoes.

CREAM OF CHICKEN SOUP

**A favourite of ours –
gets your insides dancing**

**SERVES 6
COSTS £2.50**

INGREDIENTS
1.5l chicken stock (see page 122) or 2 stock cubes
500mls double cream
4oz butter
4oz flour

EQUIPMENT
Saucepan, whisk, wooden spoon, measuring jug

1. This is great with bits of leftover chicken in... Put the stock and cream in a saucepan (if you're making fresh stock, have a look at our recipe on page 122. You can shred the chicken from the carcass and put it back in the soup as you make this).

2. Place the butter in another saucepan and melt. Add the flour and make into a roux mixture.

3. Slowly add a little of the roux mixture to the stock, bit by bit until it's all added, creating a soup consistency. Serve with warmed bread.

SAUSAGE WITH MUSTARD MASH AND ONION GRAVY

**SERVES 2
COSTS £2.50**

INGREDIENTS
350ml brown chicken stock (see page 122) or stock cube
2 tbls sunflower oil
400g or 4 small onions
1 tsp plain flour
1 tsp red currant jelly
2 large potatoes, peeled and diced
1 tbls course grain mustard
2 Cumberland sausages

EQUIPMENT
Sharp knife, chopping board, saucepans x 2, baking tray, peeler, wooden spoon, sieve, potato masher

1. To make the onion gravy, heat a saucepan with 2 tbls oil and add the onion and cook for about 10 minutes on a medium heat. Add the flour and cook for further 2 minutes, stirring continuously and being careful not to burn the bottom of the pan. Add the brown chicken stock (see page 122), and 1 tsp red currant jelly and reduce to a thick gravy. This will take about 10 minutes.

2. Place the sausages on a baking tray and place in a pre-heated oven at gas mark 4 / 180°C and cook for 10 – 15 mins or until cooked through.

3. Place the diced potatoes in a pan; cover with water and bring to boil. When cooked, drain and mash then add the mustard. Add salt and pepper to taste.

*Big juicy bangers. Creamy mash.
Onion gravy, and a smattering of peas.
Mmmm*

LANCASHIRE HOT POT

SERVES 2
COSTS £4

INGREDIENTS
400g neck of lamb, cut into 2cm cubes
1 tbls plain flour
3 tbls olive oil
1 medium onion, finely sliced
1 carrot, peeled and sliced
1 tbls thyme, chopped
1 tbls rosemary, chopped
1 clove garlic, chopped
2 large floury potatoes, peeled and thinly sliced
20g butter
500ml homemade chicken stock, or chicken stock if you have any
– if not we'd use Knorr cubes
salt and pepper

EQUIPMENT
Sharp knife, a measuring jug, a mixing bowl,
an ovenproof pan or casserole dish

1. Place the lamb into a bowl and add the flour – mix well
and season with pepper. Heat an ovenproof pan and add
1 tbls olive oil. Fry the onions, carrot and garlic until lightly
browned, then remove to a bowl and set aside.

2. In the same pan, fry the lamb with the remaining olive
oil until browned and add to the bowl with the onions.
Remove any excess fat from the pan.

3. Mix the lamb, onions and carrot, then layer back into
the pan, seasoning each layer with salt, pepper, rosemary,
thyme and the stock. Arrange the potatoes neatly over the
top, put the lid onto the pan and cook in a pre-heated oven
gas mark 2 / 150°C for 1 ½ hours, then remove the lid and
cook for a further 30 minutes. Season to taste and serve.

> **Pure comfort in a pot. That's hot pot...**
> **Reet good scran!!**

SAUSAGE ROLLS

Make a load and freeze them

SERVES 4
COSTS £3

INGREDIENTS
300g sausage meat
1 egg yolk
1 egg beaten
1 onion, finely chopped
1 crushed clove garlic
80g fresh breadcrumbs
3 tbls chopped parsley
3 tbls chopped thyme
salt and pepper to season
10 x 5cm rectangle frozen puff pastry, x4

EQUIPMENT
Sharp knife, chopping board, frying pan, saucepan,
baking tray, peeler, rolling pin, mixing bowl, wooden
spoon, whisk, blender, fork, sieve or colander, skewer,
grater, hand blender, potato masher, pastry brush

1. Place all of the ingredients in a bowl and add one
egg yolk. Mix thoroughly and split into four balls.

2. Roll out into a sausage shape. Wrap the pastry around
the meat.

3. Brush the beaten egg onto the sausage rolls and place
in pre-heated oven at gas mark 6 / 200°C for 15 minutes or
until brown. Serve.

The opposing forces of yin and yang are reflected in Chinese cooking as much as Chinese life. Recipes are traditionally based on opposites, balancing hot with cold, pickled with fresh and spicy with mild.

While many of the dishes you'll see in the takeaway are British adaptations, the flavours of Chinese food – garlic, ginger, sesame, cloves, cinnamon, fennel, star anise and pepper – are classic tastes, feeding the Chinese for centuries...

CHINE

Twice the taste and not a deep fat fryer in sight

VEGETABLE SPRING ROLLS

SERVES 4
COSTS £4

	Each portion contains		
CALS 203	**FAT** 12g	**SALT** 0.8g
11%	15%	12%
of an adults' guideline daily amount		

INGREDIENTS
50g vermicelli noodles
4 mushrooms, thinly sliced
1 tbsp groundnut oil
2 medium carrots, peeled and cut into fine strips
125g mangetout, cut lengthways into fine strips
3 spring onions, trimmed and chopped
125g beansprouts
½ inch fresh ginger, peeled and grated
1 tbsp light soy sauce
1 egg, separated
salt and freshly ground pepper
20 spring roll wrappers, each about 12cm square
vegetable oil for frying

EQUIPMENT
Bowl, wok or frying pan, baking tray, sharp knife

1. Put the vermicelli in a bowl and pour over enough boiling water to cover. Leave to soak for 5 minutes or until softened, then drain – cut into 10cm lengths.

2. Heat a wok or large frying pan, add the groundnut oil and, when hot, add carrots and stir fry for 1 minute. Add the mangetout and spring onions and stir fry for 2 – 3 minutes. Tip the vegetables into a bowl and leave to cool.

3. Stir the vermicelli and mushrooms into the cooled vegetables with the beansprouts, ginger, soy sauce and egg yolk. Season with salt and pepper and mix thoroughly.

4. Brush the edges of the spring roll wrappers with a little beaten egg white. Spoon 2 teaspoons of the vegetable filling on to the wrapper in 7cm log shape. Fold the wrapper edge over the filling, and then fold in the right and left sides. Brush the folded edges with more egg white and roll up neatly. Place on an oiled baking sheet, seam-side down and make the rest of the spring rolls.

5. Heat the oil in a frying pan and shallow fry, turning every two minutes until golden brown. Drain on absorbent kitchen paper and serve.

SUI MAI

MAKES 20 PORTIONS – SERVE AS A STARTER
COSTS £4

INGREDIENTS
75g canned water chestnuts, drained and finely chopped
75g raw prawns, coarsely chopped
175g fresh pork mince
1 tbls smoked bacon, finely chopped
½ tbls light soy sauce plus extra to serve
1 tsp dark soy sauce
½ tbls Chinese rice wine
1 tbls fresh root ginger, finely chopped
2 spring onions, trimmed and finely chopped
1 tsp sesame oil
1 egg white lightly beaten
salt and pepper
20 wonton skins, thawed if frozen
toasted sesame seeds to garnish

EQUIPMENT
Sharp knife, chopping board, saucepan, mixing bowl, wooden spoon, whisk

1. Put the water chestnuts, prawns, pork mince and bacon in a bowl and mix together. Add the soy sauces, Chinese rice wine, ginger, spring onion, sesame oil and egg. Season with salt and pepper.

2. Place a spoonful of filling in the centre of a wonton skin. Bring the sides up and press down to make a basket shape. Flatten the base so the wonton stands solid – the top should be wide open, exposing the filling.

3. Put the parcels on a heatproof plate or wire rack inside a wok or saucepan, half filled with boiling water. Cover then steam for about 20 minutes. Drizzle with soy sauce and serve with sesame seeds.

10 minutes to prepare,
10 minutes to steam,
2 minutes to eat.

CHICKEN AND SWEETCORN SOUP

SERVES 2
COSTS £2.50

INGREDIENTS
400g or 1 can of creamed sweetcorn
400ml chicken stock or chicken stock cube
50g chicken thigh, diced
¼ tsp fresh ginger
½ tsp sesame oil
10g cornflour
1 tsp light soy sauce
1 egg white, whisked
1 spring onion

EQUIPMENT
Sharp knife, chopping board, frying pan, saucepan, baking tray, peeler, rolling pin, mixing bowl, wooden spoon, whisk, blender, fork, sieve or colander, skewer, grater, hand blender, potato masher, pastry brush

1. Bring the stock to boil before adding the ginger, diced chicken, soy sauce and sweetcorn.

2. Mix the cornflour with water, then mix into the stock until you achieve the correct consistency.

3. Add the whisked egg white to hot soup until the egg white is cooked.

BEEF WITH GREEN PEPPERS IN BLACK BEAN SAUCE

SERVES 2
COSTS £3

INGREDIENTS
250g rump steak, sliced
3 tbls sunflower oil
½ onion, peeled and sliced
½ green pepper, cored and sliced
1 clove garlic, finely chopped
1 tsp light soy sauce
1 tbls oyster sauce
½ tsp sesame oil
½ tsp caster sugar
2 tbls black bean sauce
1 tsp cornflour mixed with 100ml water

EQUIPMENT
Large frying pan or wok, wooden spoon, mixing bowl, measuring jug, sharp knife

1. Heat a large frying pan or wok with the 1 tbls of sunflower oil until very hot, then add the beef and stir fry for about 2 minutes until it has a nice colour. Remove it from the pan and set aside on a plate.

2. Heat the pan with the remaining sunflower oil and stir fry the onions, garlic and peppers for 2 minutes, then add the beef again. Add the soy, oyster and black bean sauce and continue to cook for 1 minute.

3. Add the sugar and the cornflour mix and stir well, before stirring in the sesame oil and serving.

Be careful not to over-fry the beef...

SALT AND PEPPER CHICKEN WINGS

One to share, simply addictive...

SERVES 4
COSTS £1.50

INGREDIENTS
1kg chicken wings
2 tbls spice mix (see page 123)
1 red chilli
2 cloves garlic
5cm piece of ginger, peeled and finely sliced

EQUIPMENT
Baking tray, mixing bowl, wire rack

1. Place the chicken wings in a bowl — add the spice mix and cover wings thoroughly.

2. Put the wings on a wire rack over a roasting tin, then cook them in the oven, gas mark 4 / 180°C and cook for 25 – 30 minutes until crisp and golden.

3. Serve with salad.

Each portion contains		
CALS 186	**FAT** 12g	**SALT** 1.2g
9%	15%	20%
of an adults' guideline daily amount		

10 MINUTE CHILLI BEEF NOODLES

SERVES 2
COSTS £2.80

INGREDIENTS
250g dried eggs noodles
250g rump steak, sliced about 1cm thick
1 tsp cornflour
2 tsp sesame oil
1 tsp grated ginger
1 clove garlic, crushed
1 large red pepper, deseeded and sliced
3 carrots peeled and cut into matchsticks
100g mangetout, sliced
3 tbls sweet chilli sauce
1 tbls light soy sauce

EQUIPMENT
Large pan, grater, sharp knife, wooden spoon

1. Cook the noodles in a large pan of water according to the packet instructions, then run the cold tap over them to cool and drain. Toss the strips of steak in the cornflour.

2. Heat the oil in a wok or frying pan until almost smoking. Add the steak, ginger and garlic and stir-fry over a high heat for 1 – 2 minutes until the steak is browned all over (if you overcook the beef it will become chewy).

3. Add the pepper, carrots, mangetout and soy sauce to the pan and stir-fry for 3 minutes. Stir in the chilli sauce and cook for a further minute, then stir in the noodles and the sesame oil and serve in bowls.

You choose how hot

STIR FRIED LEMON CHICKEN

Juicy chicken, tangy sauce.
Plenty to mix your rice up with.

MAKES 2 PORTIONS
COSTS £4

INGREDIENTS
2 chicken fillets, cut into thin strips
1 egg white
3 tsp cornflour
2 tbls sunflower oil
50mls chicken stock
2 tbls fresh lemon juice
1 tbls light soy sauce
1 tbls Chinese rice wine
1 tbls sugar
2 garlic cloves
¼ tsp chilli flakes

EQUIPMENT
Sharp knife, chopping board, frying pan, saucepan,
mixing bowl, whisk

1. Lightly whisk the egg white and 1 tsp cornflour until
smooth. Pour the mixture over the chicken strips and mix
well until coated evenly. Leave to marinate in refrigerator
for at least 20 minutes.

2. Heat the oil in a large frying pan and add the chicken.
Stirfry for 1 – 2 minutes or until the chicken has turned
white. Set the chicken aside.

3. Heat a frying pan and add the chicken stock, lemon
juice, soy sauce, Chinese rice wine, sugar, garlic and chilli
flakes, and bring to the boil. Blend the remaining cornflour
with a tbls water and stir in stock. Simmer for 1 minute.

4. Return the chicken to the frying pan, simmer for a further
2 – 3 minutes or until the chicken is tender and the sauce
has thickened. Serve immediately with boiled rice.

PRAWN CHOW MEIN

SERVES 2
COSTS £4

INGREDIENTS
250g large peeled raw prawns
225g dried egg noodles
3 tbls sunflower oil
1 yellow pepper, deseeded and sliced
100g button mushrooms, sliced
6 spring onions, shredded
100g beansprouts
2 cloves garlic, crushed
2 tsp grated ginger
2 tbls light soy sauce
1 tbls oyster sauce
½ tsp Chinese five spice
2 tbls rice wine or sherry
2 tsp cornflour mixed with 2 tbls water

EQUIPMENT
Large frying pan or wok, large saucepan, wooden spoon,
mixing bowl, measuring jug, sharp knife

1. Bring a large pan of water to the boil and cook the egg
noodles as stated on the packet – usually about 4 – 5
minutes for medium egg noodles. Put the pan into an
empty sink and allow the cold water to run over the
noodles to cool, then drain and set aside.

2. Heat a large frying pan with the sunflower oil until very
hot; add the pepper, mushrooms, ginger and garlic and
stir-fry for 2 minutes. Add the prawns and continue to cook
for 1 minute. Finally, add the beansprouts, noodles, oyster
sauce, soy and five spice and continue to cook for 1 minute.

3. Add the rice wine and cornflour mix, stir in the spring
onions and serve.

BANG BANG CHICKEN

SERVES 2 AS A MAIN COURSE / 4 AS A STARTER
COSTS £4

INGREDIENTS
2 skinless chicken breasts or leftover chicken
1 tbls soy sauce
1 chilli
200g peanut butter
4 tbls sweet chilli sauce
4 tbls sesame oil
2 tbls vegetable oil
1 tsp chilli oil
1 baby gem, shredded
1 carrot, peeled and finely cut
3 spring onion, sliced
1 red onion, finely sliced
50g beansprouts
2 tbls olive oil
juice of 1 lime
2 tbls coriander

EQUIPMENT
Sharp knife, chopping board, saucepan, mixing bowl, wooden spoon, whisk

1. Put the chicken, soy sauce and half chilli in the saucepan. Cover with cold water and bring to the boil and simmer for 5 – 10 minutes until the chicken is cooked through. Take off the heat and leave to cool for 10 minutes.

2. To make the sauce, place the peanut butter, sweet chilli, sesame, vegetable and chilli oil in a bowl and whisk until fully mixed.

3. To make the salad, add the baby gem, carrot, spring onion, red onion, and the beansprout in a bowl and mix with olive oil and lime.

4. When the chicken is cool, slice it thinly, place on top of the salad, pour the sauce over and serve.

DUCK PANCAKES

SERVES 2
COSTS £4

INGREDIENTS
duck legs x 2
6 spring roll wrappers
¼ cucumber, cored and sliced thinly
3 spring onions, shredded
6 peppercorns
2 tbls dark soy sauce
1 star anise
3 tbls hoi sin sauce

Each portion contains		
CALS	**FAT**	**SALT**
375	5g	2.2g
19%	7%	36%
of an adults' guideline daily amount		

EQUIPMENT
Saucepan, measuring spoons, mixing bowl

1. Place the peppercorns, star anise and soy sauce in a saucepan. Add the water or stock and duck legs. Bring to the boil then simmer for about one hour, or until the duck meat is tender. Leave the duck legs to cool down in the stock.

2. Once cooled, take the duck legs out – remove the skin and shred the meat using your fingers. Put in a bowl and mix with the cucumber and spring onion.

3. Place the mixture in the middle of the pancake wrapper and divide the hoi sin sauce between the wraps. Roll up and enjoy.

Make them with the sui mais on page 33

Greek food shares many of its flavours with other Mediterranean countries, including Italy, Turkey and the Balkans. Herbs include oregano, mint, garlic, onion, dill, basil, bay laurel and thyme, plus gallons of olive oil, pressed from the olive orchards that cover acres of hillside.

Greece's long coastline lends itself to plenty of fish dishes, and its mountainous terrain often puts lamb on the menu. But we'd be doing Greece a disservice by not mentioning yoghurt, feta and pitta – a pre-requisite for the iconic kebab.

E AND FETA
STUFFED PEPPERS

SERVES 2 – 3
COSTS £3.80

INGREDIENTS
1 each yellow, green and red peppers
1 medium onion, peeled and finely diced
1 clove garlic, crushed
1 tsp ground cumin
2 tbls olive oil
½ tsp dried mint
½ tsp dried oregano
2 tomatoes, deseeded and diced
250g long grain rice (uncooked weight), cooked and cooled
30g raisins
30g pine nuts
40g feta cheese

EQUIPMENT
Frying pan, wooden spoon, sharp knife,
baking tray, mixing bowl

1. Slice the peppers in half lengthways and remove the seeds, then place on a baking tray and set aside.

2. Heat a frying pan with the olive oil and fry the onions over a medium heat for about 5 minutes until soft. Add the garlic, ground cumin, mint, oregano and diced tomatoes and continue to cook for 1 minute.

3. Place the cooked rice in a mixing bowl and add the onion and tomato mixture, raisins, pine nuts and feta cheese and mix well. Season to taste with salt and pepper and then fill the peppers with the mixture.

4. Place the peppers into a pre-heated oven gas mark 6 / 200°C for about 20 – 25 minutes, or until the peppers have softened.

5. Remove from the oven and serve with salad leaves.

> **The Greek Goddess of vegetarian food**

MOUSSAKA

> **Let the mouss-loose!**

SERVES 4
COSTS £4

INGREDIENTS
175g grated parmesan or cheddar (or a mix)
small onion, diced
1¾ pints of semi skimmed milk
60g butter
60g flour
2 cloves
a sprig of rosemary
4 tbls sunflower oil
1 medium aubergine, thinly sliced
1 medium onion, finely chopped
1 glove garlic, crushed
¼ tsp all spice
½ tsp ground cinnamon
375g lamb mince
200g can of chopped tomato
1 tbls tomato puree

EQUIPMENT
Saucepan, overproof dish, wooden spoon

1. To make the cheese sauce, put the onion, milk, cloves and rosemary in a saucepan. Bring to the boil and simmer gently for about 10 minutes, letting the milk infuse.

2. Heat 2 tbls oil in a frying pan. Add the onion and cook until it softens – add the garlic, all spice and cinnamon and cook for another minute. Add the lamb and cook until browned, before adding the tomatoes, tomato puree and a slash of water and simmer on a low heat for 30 minutes.

3. Brush the aubergine with oil and season. Griddle until cooked or put it under a grill on a medium heat.

4. Place one layer of aubergine on the bottom of an oven proof dish then layer with the mince. Add another layer of aubergine and repeat this process until the ingredients have filled the dish. Finally, top with cheese sauce and place in pre-heated oven at gas mark 4 / 180°C for 40 minutes. Let your moussaka stand for 10 minutes before serving.

LAMB WITH HUMOUS AND FLAT BREAD

SERVES 4
COSTS £2.20

INGREDIENTS
200g minced lamb
2 tbls unsalted peanuts, chopped
½ tsp smoked paprika
4 large tbls humous
2 tbls fresh parsley, chopped
salt and pepper to taste
4 small flat breads

EQUIPMENT
Frying pan, food processor, sharp knife, wooden spoon

1. Heat a frying pan with 3 tbls olive oil and fry the onions over a medium heat for about 7 minutes until golden brown. Remove from the pan and set aside.

2. Heat the frying pan again and add the lamb, then cook over a medium to high heat, breaking up the lamb with a fork until the lamb is golden and crisp. Add the peanuts, onions, ground cinnamon and ground cumin. Mix well and season to taste.

3. Warm the flatbreads and serve them on a plate with the humous spread over them. Scatter the lamb on top, followed by the parsley and smoked paprika.

Enough for you and your friends – it works with a curry too

HUMOUS

SERVES 6 AS A DIP
COSTS £1.50

INGREDIENTS
400g tinned chickpeas, drained
1 lemon, juice and zest
2 tbls tahini
2 cloves garlic, peeled
120ml olive oil
salt

EQUIPMENT
Sharp knife, chopping board, blender, sieve or colander, grater

1. Put the chickpeas in a food processor with the garlic, lemon juice and zest, tahini and salt. Whizz together and pour in the olive oil as the motor is still running.

2. You want a smooth dip, so add cold water if necessary – still with the motor running – until you get the consistency you want. Taste for flavour and add a bit more salt if necessary.

3. Serve as a dip with hot pitta bread, vegetable crudités or with jacket potatoes.

We've yet to find anyone who doesn't like this dip

CHICKEN KEBAB AND GREEK SALAD

SERVES 2
COSTS £2.50

INGREDIENTS
For the kebab:
1 large chicken breast, sliced into 6 strips
¼ white onion, grated
2 cloves garlic, crushed
1 tsp ground cumin
½ tsp smoked paprika
3 tbls olive oil
juice from ½ lemon
2 flat breads or 2 pitta bread

Each portion contains		
CALS 419	**FAT** 14g	**SALT** 1.4g
22%	19%	24%
of an adults' guideline daily amount		

For the Greek salad:
½ little gem lettuce, shredded
½ yellow pepper, diced
5 cherry tomatoes, halved
½ small red onion, peeled and diced
8cm piece of cucumber, cored and diced
30g feta cheese
2 tbls olive oil
juice from ½ lemon
1 tsp dried oregano
black pepper to taste

EQUIPMENT
Baking tray, 2 mixing bowls, grater, sharp knife

1. For the kebab: mix together the chicken, grated onion, garlic, cumin, paprika and olive oil in a bowl, then season with black pepper and marinate for at least 30 minutes.

2. For the Greek salad: mix together the little gem, yellow pepper, tomatoes, cucumber, red onion, lemon juice, olive oil and oregano. Season with black pepper; set aside.

3. Heat up the grill and place the marinated chicken on a baking tray – grill for about 3 minutes on each side until cooked. Remove; season with a little salt and keep warm.

4. Place the flatbreads or pittas under the grill to warm through, then divide the Greek salad between the two and lay the chicken over it. Crumble the feta cheese over the chicken, roll up and serve.

Warm comforting food

VEGETABLE KEBAB

Towards your five a day

SERVES 4
COSTS £3.50

INGREDIENTS
1 courgette, cut into 1cm chunks
1 green pepper, cut into 1cm chunks
8 cherry tomatoes
1 red onion, peeled and chopped into large chunks
8 button mushrooms
1 tbls smoked paprika
2 tsp ground cumin
2 cloves garlic, crushed
4 tbls olive oil
juice from ½ lemon
½ iceberg lettuce, shredded
4 pitta breads
3 tbls yogurt
salt and pepper

EQUIPMENT
Baking tray, mixing bowl, 4 wooden skewers, sharp knife

1. Place the courgettes, green pepper, cherry tomatoes and red onion in a bowl and add the paprika, cumin, garlic, olive oil and lemon juice. Mix well and leave to marinate for at least 30 minutes.

2. After 30 minutes, divide the vegetables between the 4 skewers by threading them onto each one evenly, then lay the skewers on a baking tray. Season with salt and pepper and place into a pre-heated oven at gas mark 6 / 200°C for about 20 minutes, turning once or until the vegetables are soft and golden.

3. To serve, toast the pitta breads and slice them open, then divide the iceberg lettuce between them. Place 1 vegetable skewer in each, then finish with a dollop of yoghurt.

Definitely worth the effort

SPICY LAMB PITTAS

SERVES 3
COSTS £3.50

INGREDIENTS
300g minced lamb
2 tbls olive oil
1 clove garlic, crushed
1 small onion, peeled and grated
1 tbls mango chutney
1 tsp grated ginger
1 long green chillies, chopped
½ tsp ground cumin
½ tsp ground coriander
salt and pepper to taste
3 pitta bread
6 spring onions, shredded
3 tomatoes, roughly chopped
½ little gem, shredded
2 tbls fresh coriander, chopped
1 tbls fresh mint, chopped
3 tbls natural yoghurt

EQUIPMENT
2 mixing bowls, frying pan, wooden spoon, sharp knife

1. Put the lamb mince in a bowl along with the garlic, grated onion, mango chutney, ginger, cumin, green chillies and ground coriander. Season with a little salt and pepper. Combine the mixture well, either in a food processor or by hand. Shape the mixture into 6 small burgers, then place in the fridge for at least 30 minutes.

2. Combine the spring onion, tomatoes, little gem, coriander and mint in a bowl, then set aside.

3. Heat your grill and cook the lamb under a medium heat for about 6 minutes turning 3 – 4 times during cooking. While the burgers are cooking, toast the pitta breads, then divide the tomato mixture between the 3 and place 2 burgers in each.

4. Finish with a spoon of yoghurt in each one and serve.

GRILLED SARDINES WITH GREEK SALAD

SERVES 2
COSTS £3.50

INGREDIENTS
½ little gem lettuce, shredded
½ yellow pepper, diced
5 cherry tomatoes, halved
½ small red onion, peeled and diced
½ tsp red wine vinegar
8cm piece of cucumber, cored and diced
30g feta cheese
3 tbls olive oil
juice from ½ lemon
1 tsp dried oregano
4 sardines
black pepper to taste

EQUIPMENT
Baking tray, mixing bowls, sharp knife

1. For the sardines: place the sardines on a baking tray and brush with 1 tbls of the olive oil, then season and sprinkle over the rosemary. Set aside.

2. For the Greek salad: mix together the little gem, yellow pepper, tomatoes, cucumber, red onion, lemon juice, red wine vinegar, 2 tbls olive oil and oregano in a bowl. Season with a little black pepper, then set aside.

3. Heat the grill to its highest setting and cook the sardines for about 3 – 4 minutes on each side, or until cooked through. They should be crisp but not burnt.

4. To serve, divide the Greek salad between 2 plates and place 2 sardines on each.

Not exactly in every takeaway but sardines are cheap, easy to cook and full of Omega 3s. Brain food, you know.

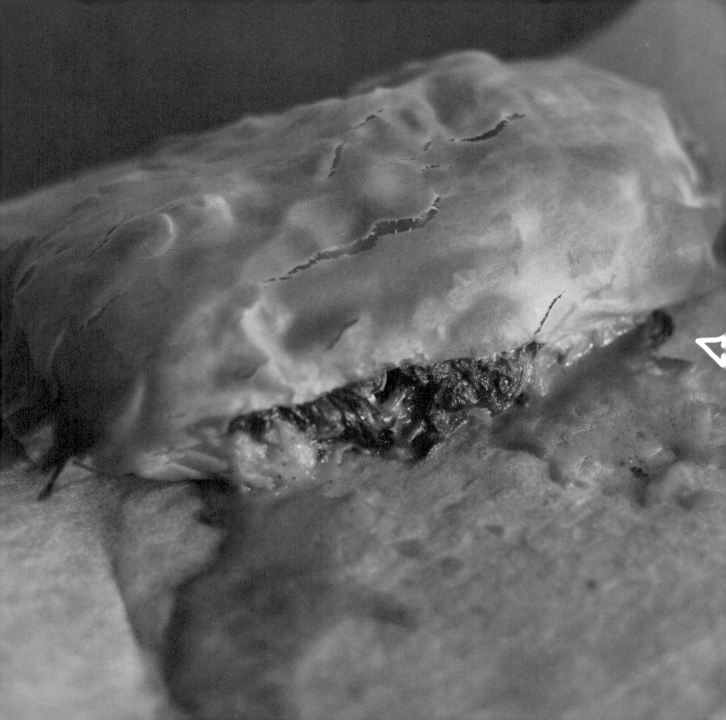

FETA AND SPINACH PARCELS

SERVES 2 – 4
COSTS £3

INGREDIENTS
1 small onion, diced
1 clove garlic, chopped
1 tsp fresh thyme
½ leek, finely sliced
150g spinach
40g feta, grated
2 tbls sunflower oil
2 sheets of filo pastry

EQUIPMENT
Sharp knife, chopping board, saucepan, baking tray, wooden spoon, pastry brush, grater

1. Heat the oil in a pan on a medium heat, adding the onion, garlic and leek. Cook for 2 – 3 minutes until soft, then add the thyme, spinach and grated feta. Cook for 2 minutes until the spinach has wilted. Take off heat and leave to cool slightly.

2. Cut in half 3 sheets of filo pastry – put the mix in the middle of one square and fold to create a parcel.

3. Place on a baking tray and put in a pre-heated oven at gas mark 4 / 180°C for 15 – 20 minutes or until golden brown. Serve with salad.

What's not to love about these cheesy puffs?

LAMB KEBAB

Two hands needed.
Consider yourself warned…

SERVES 2
COSTS £2.50

INGREDIENTS
For the kebab:
200g lamb leg steak, sliced to about 2cm thick
¼ onion, grated
2 cloves garlic, crushed
1 tsp ground cumin
1 tsp paprika
1 tsp ground coriander
2 tsp dried mint
3 tbls olive oil
juice from ½ lemon
2 pitta bread

For the salad:
handful mixed salad leaves
2 tbls finely shredded white cabbage
½ small red onion peeled and finely sliced
juice from ½ lemon

EQUIPMENT
Baking tray, 2 mixing bowls, grater, sharp knife

1. In a bowl, mix together the lamb, grated onion, garlic, cumin, coriander, mint, paprika and olive oil, then season with a little black pepper and leave to marinate for at least 30 minutes.

2. Heat up the grill and place the marinated lamb on a baking tray and grill for about 3 minutes on each side. Remove from the heat and season with a little salt – keep warm in a low oven.

3. Place the salad leaves, cabbage, red onion and lemon juice into a bowl and mix well, then warm the pitta bread and divide the salad between the two. Lay the lamb over it and serve.

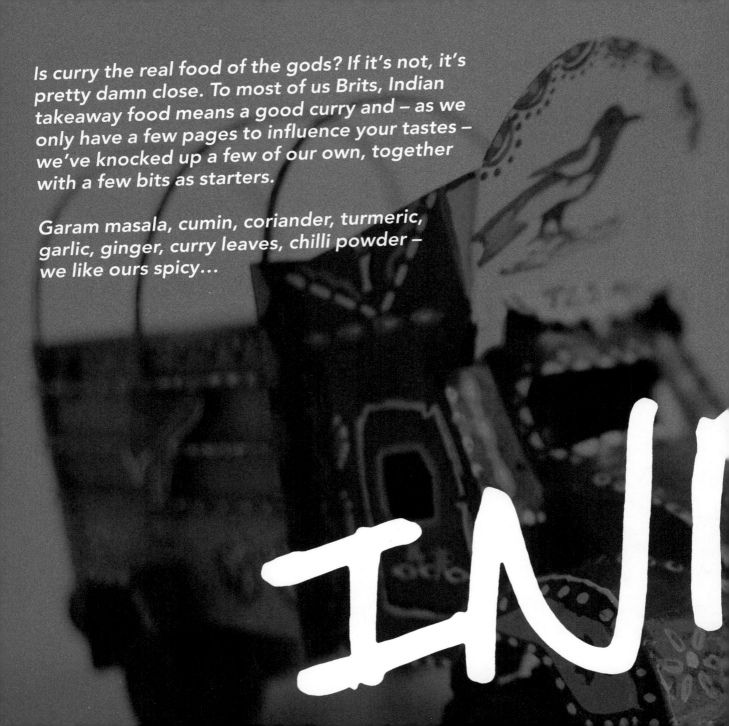

Is curry the real food of the gods? If it's not, it's pretty damn close. To most of us Brits, Indian takeaway food means a good curry and – as we only have a few pages to influence your tastes – we've knocked up a few of our own, together with a few bits as starters.

Garam masala, cumin, coriander, turmeric, garlic, ginger, curry leaves, chilli powder – we like ours spicy…

IN

Scrummy savoury parcels

POTATO AND PEA SAMOSA

SERVES 6
COSTS £2.50

INGREDIENTS
For the samosas:
2 tbls sunflower oil
¼ tsp black mustard seeds
100g finely diced onions
½ tsp finely grated ginger
30g frozen peas
½ tbls ground coriander
½ tsp cumin seeds
1 small green chilli, finely diced
1 clove garlic, crushed
¼ tsp ground turmeric
300g potatoes cooked and lightly crushed
2 tbls fresh coriander, chopped
10 sheets of filo pastry
5 tbls melted butter
salt and pepper

For the raita:
250ml natural yogurt
½ cucumber, deseeded and finely diced
large handful fresh mint leaves, chopped
pinch of salt

Each portion contains

CALS	FAT	SALT
272	7g	0.8g
14%	10%	13%

of an adults' guideline daily amount

EQUIPMENT
Frying pan, baking trays, pastry brush, small bowl, grater, sharp knife

1. Heat a frying pan and add the oil. Fry the mustard seeds for about 10 seconds and then add the onions, garlic and ginger and cook for 2 – 3 minutes on a high heat. Add the peas, fresh chilli and spices and continue to cook for 30 seconds. Then add a splash of water, cook for 1 minute and add the potatoes and fresh coriander and cook for 2 more minutes. Season to taste and tip onto a flat tray to cool.

2. Unroll the pastry and cover with a clean damp tea towel. Take one sheet of pastry and brush it with melted butter, then fold in one third of the pastry lengthways into the centre, brush this piece with butter and fold the other side in to leave a long triple layered strip.

3. Place one large teaspoon of the filling at one end of the strip, leaving a 2cm border. Take the right corner and fold diagonally to the left, enclosing the filling and forming a triangle. Fold again along the crease and continue to do this until you reach the end. Brush with a little more butter and place onto a baking tray lined with greaseproof paper, then repeat the process with the rest of the mixture.

4. Bake in a pre-heated oven gas mark 6 / 200°C for 30 – 35 minutes turning over once during cooking until they're golden.

5. While cooking mix the ingredients for the raita and serve the samosas with the raita.

TARKA DHAL

SERVES 4 AS A SIDE
COSTS £1.75

INGREDIENTS
For the dhal:
225g red lentils (masoor dhal)
2 tbls sunflower oil
1 small onion, peeled and thinly sliced
1 tsp ground turmeric
½ tsp ground black pepper
500ml water
1 green chilli, finely chopped
2 tsp grated ginger
salt to taste
1 tbls fresh coriander, chopped

For the tarka:
1 tbls sunflower oil
8 curry leaves (now widely available)
2 cloves garlic, peeled and thinly sliced
½ small onion, peeled and thinly sliced
1 green chilli, finely diced
1 tsp ground coriander

EQUIPMENT
Large pan, frying pan, wooden spoon, grater, sharp knife, measuring jug

Making the dhal:
1. Heat 2 tbls oil in a large pan and add the onions and garlic; cook over a medium heat for about 3 minutes. Add the ginger, turmeric, pepper and lentils and stir well.

Making the tarka:
2. Add the water and chillies, then bring to the boil. Turn the heat down and simmer with the lid on for 20 minutes or until the lentils are cooked and look a bit mushy.

3. Heat 1 tbls oil in a frying pan and add the onions; cook over a medium to high heat for 2 minutes then add the garlic and continue to cook for 1 minute before adding the curry leaves, green chilli and ground coriander. Cook for another minute and then pour the mixture into the lentils.

4. Season the lentils with salt to taste and mix well, then stir in the fresh coriander and serve.

> Very tasty as it is or be brave and add different spices – you can create loads with this basic dhal dish

CHICKEN TIKKA MASALA

Not for nothing is the humble chicken tikka the nation's favourite dish

SERVES 2
COSTS £3 INCLUDING RICE

INGREDIENTS
350g chicken breasts, cut into 2cm cubes
2 tbls plain yogurt (0% fat)
1 clove garlic, crushed
1 tsp grated ginger
¼ tsp chilli powder
1½ tsp paprika
¼ tsp ground coriander
¼ tsp ground cumin
½ tsp garam masala
juice from ½ lime
200ml passata
¼ tsp ground fenugreek
2 tbls fresh coriander, chopped
½ tsp salt

Each portion contains		
CALS 469	**FAT** 7g	**SALT** 1g
24%	10%	18%
of an adults' guideline daily amount		

EQUIPMENT
Mixing bowl, large saucepan, small saucepan, sharp knife

1. In a bowl, mix together the yogurt, garlic, ginger, chilli powder, 1 tsp of the paprika, ground coriander, ground cumin, ½ tsp of the garam masala, lime juice and a pinch of salt. Add the chicken, mix well and leave to marinate for 30 minutes at room temperature or two hours in the fridge.

2. Heat a large pan and add the chicken, the marinade, and cook on a medium heat for about ten minutes until the chicken is cooked and tender. You'll need to keep stirring to make sure it doesn't stick.

3. In a small pan, add the passata, ground fenugreek, 1 tsp paprika and ½ tsp garam masala and cook for about 3 minutes until hot.

4. Now stir the tomato sauce into the chicken, add the coriander, season to taste with salt and mix well. Serve with pilau or basmati rice.

KEEMA RICE

SERVES 2
COSTS £1.30

INGREDIENTS
225g basmati rice
300ml hot water
100g minced lamb
½ tsp ground cumin
½ tsp ground coriander
1 tsp ground turmeric
¼ tsp ground fenugreek
1 long red chilli, finely diced
1 small clove garlic, crushed
2 tsp ginger grated

EQUIPMENT
Large saucepan, circle of greaseproof paper, frying pan, sharp knife, wooden spoon, measuring jug, grater, colander

1. Put the rice in a bowl and wash in several changes of cold water, then leave to soak for 20 minutes and drain into a colander.

2. Put the rice in a saucepan and pour over the hot water. Bring to the boil, then stir and cover with a circle of greaseproof paper and a tight fitting lid. Reduce the heat to its lowest setting and cook without removing the lid for ten minutes.

3. After ten minutes remove from the heat and leave for a further five minutes without removing the lid. (Don't have a peek – it will be OK!)

4. While the rice is cooking, heat a frying pan; add the minced lamb and cook for about five minutes until the meat is golden. Now add all of the dry spices, the garlic, chilli and ginger and continue to cook for 30 seconds being careful not to burn them.

5. When the rice is cooked, remove the lid and use a fork to fluff it up. Add the lamb mixture along with the fresh coriander and season to taste with salt.

Meaty rice? Mmmm... and it couldn't be easier to make

We all need a bit of good korma!

CHICKEN KORMA

SERVES 4
COSTS £6

Each portion contains		
CALS 443	**FAT** 20g	**SALT** 1.4g
23%	27%	24%
of an adults' guideline daily amount		

INGREDIENTS
5cm cinnamon stick
8 cardamom pods, seeds crushed
6 cloves
1 heaped teaspoon cumin seeds
6 tablespoons vegetable oil
3 bay leaves
130g onions, peeled and finely chopped
4cm piece fresh ginger, peeled and finely chopped
5 – 6 garlic cloves, peeled and finely chopped
1 tablespoon ground coriander
1 tablespoon ground cumin
1.5 to 2 tins chopped plum tomatoes
4 chicken breasts, skinned and cut into 2.5cm cubes
1 teaspoon medium chilli powder
salt
4 tablespoons low-fat crème fraiche
approx. 250ml water
a bunch of fresh coriander, rinsed and roughly chopped

EQUIPMENT
Chopping board, chopping knives, large frying pan, large pot, or casserole dish, small chopping knives, tablespoon measure, teaspoon measure, measuring jug, tin opener

1. Gently dry fry the cinnamon stick, crushed cardamom seeds, cloves and cumin seeds in a small frying pan, for approximately 3 minutes. Be careful not to burn the spices. Put to one side.

2. Heat the oil in a large frying pan and fry the onions for about 3 minutes. Add the ginger, garlic, bay leaves, ground cumin and ground coriander, and gently fry for 4 minutes before adding the chopped tomatoes, and bring to a gentle boil.

3. Add the chicken pieces, chilli powder, salt and approx. 250mls water and bring to the boil again. Turn the heat to medium and gently simmer for 15 minutes, turning the chicken pieces over now and then.

4. Using a pair of tongs, carefully remove the chicken pieces, and put to one side. Allow the curry to gently simmer, and reduce for a further 15 minutes.

5. Stir in the crème fraiche – the curry should thicken slightly when you do this – and add the cooked chicken pieces and fresh coriander. Bring the curry back to a gentle simmer. Check the seasoning and add a little more salt if necessary. Serve with pilau rice.

GOAN VEGETABLE CURRY

SERVES 4
COSTS £3.50

INGREDIENTS
½ aubergine, cut into 1cm cubes
1 small onion, peeled and chopped
2 tbls sunflower oil
1 large carrot, peeled and cut into 2cm cubes
100g frozen peas
2 medium potatoes, peeled and cut into 2cm cubes
1 large courgette, cut into 2cm cubes
250ml low fat coconut milk
2 large green chillies, chopped
1 clove garlic, crushed
1 tsp ginger, grated
3 tomatoes, chopped
2 tsp curry powder
1 tsp garam masala
2 tbls fresh coriander, chopped

EQUIPMENT
Large saucepan, sharp knife, wooden spoon, measuring jug, grater

1. Heat a large saucepan with the sunflower oil and cook the onions over a medium heat for about 3 minutes. Add the carrot, potato, garlic, ginger, green chillies, curry powder, garam masala and tomatoes and cook for 2 more minutes.

2. Now add the aubergine, courgettes and coconut milk and simmer with the lid on for about 15 minutes until the vegetables are tender, then add the peas and cook for 2 more minutes.

3. Add the fresh coriander and season to taste, then serve with basmati, pilau or the chana pilau rice on page 62.

Go-an 'ave a go!

CHANA PILAU

SERVES 3
COSTS £1.20

INGREDIENTS
225g basmati rice
300ml water
pinch of salt
½ white onion, finely diced
1 bay leaf
1 cinnamon stick
2 tsp fennel seeds
3 tbls oil
200g tinned chickpeas, washed and drained
½ tsp ground cumin
1 tsp paprika
½ tsp garam masala
½ tsp ground turmeric

EQUIPMENT
Bowl, large saucepan, frying pan, sharp knife

1. Put the rice in a bowl and wash with several changes of cold water – leave to soak for 20 minutes, then drain.

2. Heat 2 tbls oil in a large pan and cook the onion for about 10 minutes on a low heat until it's quite dark but not burnt, then add the bay leaf, cinnamon stick and fennel seeds and cook for 1 more minute.

3. Add the rice, water and a pinch of salt; cover and cook on a low heat for 10 minutes, then remove from the heat and leave for 5 more minutes, without removing the lid.

4. Meanwhile, heat the remaining oil in a frying pan and add the chickpeas, ground cumin, paprika, garam masala and turmeric. Gently fry for about 4 – 5 minutes, then season and stir into the rice.

PRAWN ROGAN J

SERVES 2
COSTS £5

INGREDIENTS
1 tbls sunflower oil
200g medium onion, finely diced
2 tsp grated ginger
2 cloves crushed garlic
1 tsp turmeric
4 tsp curry powder
½ tsp chilli powder
1 tsp garam masala
1 tsp fennel seeds
1 tsp cumin seeds
8 tomatoes, deseeded & quartered
250ml passata
150ml water
½ tsp salt or to taste
2 tbls natural yoghurt (0% fat)
200g large raw shelled prawns
2 tbls fresh coriander

EQUIPMENT
Large pan, measuring jug, grater, sharp knife, wooden spoon

Each portion contains		
CALS 446	**FAT** 11g	**SALT** 2.2g
23%	14%	36%
of an adults' guideline daily amount		

1. Heat a pan and add the oil, then cook the onions over a medium heat for about five minutes until they start to colour and soften. Then add the garlic, ginger, turmeric, curry powder, chilli powder, fennel seeds and cumin seeds and continue to cook for about 30 seconds.

2. Add the passata and cook on a medium heat for about ten minutes, adding a little water if it gets too thick. Add the tomato quarters and continue to cook for two minutes.

3. After two minutes add the prawns and garam masala and stir in the yogurt. Cook for a few minutes or until the prawns are cooked through; season to taste and serve with rice and naan bread.

We played with this for ages to get it just right – hope you like it

RK VINDALOO

SERVES 2
COSTS £4

INGREDIENTS
For the marinade:
700g pork leg, diced to about 2.5cm
1 tsp ground cumin
4 cardamoms, crushed
¼ tsp ground cloves
¼ tsp ground cinnamon
1 long red chilli, finely diced
1 birds eye chilli, finely diced
5cm piece of ginger, grated
4 cloves garlic, crushed
3 tbls lemon juice

For the curry:
4 tbls sunflower oil
5 cloves garlic, sliced
2 small onions, finely diced
1 tsp turmeric
½ tsp chilli powder
½ tbls tomato puree
3 tomatoes, chopped
3 tbls white wine vinegar
10 curry leaves
salt to taste
4 tbls fresh coriander, chopped

EQUIPMENT
Large pan, wooden spoon, mixing bowl, grater,
sharp knife

1. Put all of the ingredients for the marinade into a large bowl and mix well; cover and leave for at least an hour.

2. Heat the oil in a large pan and fry the onions and garlic over a medium heat for about 5 minutes until the garlic is golden and the onions are soft. Add the turmeric, chilli powder, pork and marinade and cook for 2 minutes.

3. Now add the tomato puree, chopped tomatoes, vinegar and curry leaves and cook over a low heat with the lid on, for about 1 – 1½ hours until the meat is very tender.

4. Add the chopped coriander and season with salt; serve with plain basmati or pilau rice.

A vindaloo deep in flavour – and it tastes even better the next day

ALOO GOBI

SERVES 2
COSTS £1

INGREDIENTS
1 tbls sunflower oil
1 tsp cumin seeds
1 small clove garlic, crushed
1 tsp grated ginger
2 medium potatoes, peeled and cubed
½ tsp ground turmeric
½ tsp paprika
1 tsp ground cumin
½ tsp garam masala
salt to taste
500g cauliflower
1 tbls chopped fresh coriander

EQUIPMENT
Large pan, grater, sharp knife, wooden spoon

1. Heat a pan with the oil and add the cumin seeds, garlic and ginger and cook over a medium heat for about 1 minute, before adding the potatoes, turmeric, paprika, ground cumin, garam masala, 2 tbls of water and a pinch of salt. Cover and continue cooking for about 5 minutes, stirring from time to time. Add a little more water if needed so it doesn't dry out.

2. Mix in the cauliflower and reduce the heat to low and cook with the lid on for 10 more minutes or until the potatoes and cauliflower are tender.

3. Season to taste with salt, stir in the cauliflower and serve.

This spicy veggy dish makes a nice bit on the side...

ALOO PARATHA

SERVES 8
COSTS £2

INGREDIENTS

For the filling:
1 tbls sunflower oil
2 tsp grated ginger
1 small onion, peeled and finely diced
2 cloves garlic, crushed
1 red chilli, finely diced
½ tsp ground turmeric
½ tsp chilli powder
1 tsp ground coriander
1 tsp garam masala
1 tsp black mustard seeds
2 large potatoes, boiled and lightly crushed
2 tbls fresh coriander, chopped
3 tbls sunflower oil

For the dough:
400g plain flour
½ tsp baking powder
1 tsp sugar
1 tsp salt
1 egg
220ml milk

EQUIPMENT
Saucepan, wooden spoon, mixing bowl, grater, frying pan, measuring jug, sharp knife

1. Put the flour, baking powder, salt, egg and milk in a mixing bowl and mix together to form a dough. Tip out onto a floured work top and knead for about 5 – 10 minutes until smooth, then place back into the bowl and cover with cling film and leave in a warm place to prove until it has doubled in size.

2. For the filling, heat the sunflower oil in a frying pan and cook the onion over a medium heat for about 5 minutes. Add the garlic, ginger and chilli and continue to cook for a further 1 minute. Now add the turmeric, chilli powder, ground coriander, garam masala and black mustard seeds and cook for 1 more minute.

3. Add the cooked potato, fresh coriander and season to taste with salt and pepper, then allow to cool completely.

4. Put the dough on a floured work top and divide into 8 balls. Roll out each ball to about 1½ cm thick, then place 1 tbls of the potato mixture in the middle of each and fold the edges over so that the potato is inside the dough.

5. Gently roll the potato filled dough out into a flat disc about 1 cm thick; heat a frying pan and lightly grease with sunflower oil and cook for a couple of minutes on each side until golden and serve.

NAAN BREAD

SERVES 4
COSTS 70P

INGREDIENTS
1 tsp dried active yeast
1 tsp caster sugar
2 tbls tepid water
200g plain flour
½ tsp salt
½ tsp baking powder
1 tbls sunflower oil
2 tbls plain natural yoghurt
2 tbls milk

EQUIPMENT
2 mixing bowls, large wok or baking tray, rolling pin, blowtorch

1. Mix the yeast, sugar and water in a small bowl and leave in a warm place for about 10 minutes until it starts to froth.

2. Mix the flour, salt and baking powder in a large bowl, then add the oil, yoghurt, milk and yeast mixture. Using a spoon, mix until it forms a dough and then turn out onto a worktop and knead the dough for about 10 minutes, until elastic. Put back into the bowl and cover with cling film, then leave in a warm place until it's doubled in size.

3. Take the dough out of the bowl and knead again for 1 minute, then divide into 4 balls. With a rolling pin, roll each ball into a tear shape, using a little extra flour if it sticks.

4. Turn the wok upside down and place over a hot flame on your cooker; lightly oil the top and place one of the naan breads on it. Using the blow torch, flame the top of the bread until golden and puffed. Remove and serve. If you don't want to use the wok method, heat a baking tray under a grill until very hot and place the naan dough on the baking tray, then grill until golden.

For variation, try adding 1 clove of crushed garlic and 2 tbls chopped coriander at the beginning of step 2.

Soak up yer curry or use as a base for lots of our takeaway dishes, including the lamb flatbread and chicken kebab

Italian food is based on simple taste combinations, relying on the quality of the ingredients rather than complicated recipes. Tastes include fresh vegetables – tomatoes, artichoke, asparagus and mushroom, basil, oregano and garlic, while staples like pasta, risotto rice, polenta, cheeses and olive oil pop up everywhere.

Eating out is hugely popular in Italian culture, and no meal is complete without the works – wine, coffee and lots of family...

ITA

Packed with plenty of the green stuff...

SPINACH AND CREAM CHEESE CALZONE

SERVES 2 – 4
COSTS £2

INGREDIENTS
175g strong white bread flour
1 tsp salt
1 tsp fast action dried yeast
1 tbls olive oil
120ml tepid water
200g can chopped tomatoes
1 clove garlic, crushed
1 tbls tomato puree
½ tsp caster sugar
1 tsp dried mixed herbs
200g low fat cream cheese
250g spinach
2 tbls fresh parsley, chopped

Each portion contains		
CALS 527	**FAT** 19g	**SALT** 1.8g
27%	25%	29%
of an adults' guideline daily amount		

EQUIPMENT
1 saucepan, measuring jug, wooden spoon, sharp knife, baking tray, mixing bowl

1. Make a ball of dough according to the recipe on page 123.

3. While you're waiting for the dough you can make the sauce by placing the tomatoes in a small pan along with the garlic, tomato puree, sugar and mixed herbs. Stir and heat gently until the sauce thickens slightly, then set aside. Then place the spinach in a pan with 1 tbls of water and cook until the spinach is soft, then remove from the pan and squeeze out any excess water and leave to cool.

4. When the dough is ready turn your oven on to gas mark 8 / 230°C and put a large baking tray in. Remove your dough from the bowl and place it on a lightly floured surface and bash the air back out of it, then knead again for 1 – 2 minutes and shape into a ball.

5. Flour the work surface and rolling pin and roll out the dough until it's about 28cm in diameter. Spread tomato sauce over the base, leaving about 2.5cm around the edges and dot the cream cheese, parsley and spinach all over it. Season with a little salt and lots of freshly ground black pepper.

6. Fold the calzone over into the shape of a pasty and – using a little water – seal the edges. Remove the baking tray from the oven and slide the calzone onto it and bake in the oven for 12 – 15 minutes and serve.

SPAGHETTI BOLOGNESE

SERVES 1
COSTS £1.20

INGREDIENTS
150g minced beef
2 tbls olive oil
1 small onion, peeled and finely diced
1 carrot, peeled and diced
1 stick celery, finely diced
1 clove garlic, chopped
4 mushrooms, sliced
½ glass red wine
1 tbls tomato puree
1 can chopped tomatoes
1 chicken stock cube
2 tbls fresh basil, chopped
125g spaghetti
salt and pepper to taste

EQUIPMENT
Large pan, sharp knife, wooden spoon

1. Heat a pan with 2 tbls olive oil and add the onions. Cook over a medium heat for about 4 minutes, then add the carrot, mushrooms, celery and garlic and continue to cook for 3 minutes, then remove from the pan and set aside.

2. In the same pan, cook the minced beef over the medium heat for about 5 minutes until browned. Strain off any excess fat and add the vegetable mix to the pan.

3. Now add the tomato puree and continue to cook for 1 minute, then add the red wine and cook for 2 minutes. Add the can of tomatoes and stock cube, bring to the boil and simmer for about 30 minutes, adding a little water if needed.

4. While the bolognese is cooking, bring a large pan of water to a rapid boil and cook the pasta according to the instructions on the packet. Drain into a colander in a sink.

5. Season the bolognese with salt and pepper, stir through the fresh basil and serve with the pasta.

We're not sure how much of Bologna our bolognese has seen, but it remains a rich, meaty, tomatoey favourite nonetheless…

ROAST VEGETABLE PIZZA

SERVES 2 – 4
COSTS £2.20

INGREDIENTS
200g can chopped tomatoes
1 clove garlic, crushed
1 tbls tomato puree
½ tsp caster sugar
1 tsp dried mixed herbs
1 ball mozzarella drained and torn into pieces
10 basil leaves
½ courgette diced
1 small red onion, peeled and diced
½ yellow pepper, diced
salt and pepper to taste

EQUIPMENT
Saucepan, measuring jug, wooden spoon,
sharp knife, baking tray, mixing bowl

1. Make a ball of dough according to the recipe on page 123.

2. While the dough is proving, place the courgette, pepper and red onion in a baking tray and add 2 tbls olive oil, season with salt and pepper and mix well. Bake in a pre-heated oven 200°C for about 25 – 30 minutes until cooked through, then remove and allow to cool.

3. Place the tomatoes in a small pan along with the garlic, tomato puree, sugar and mixed herbs, stir and heat gently until the sauce thickens slightly, then set aside.

4. When the dough is ready, turn your oven on to gas mark 8 / 230°C and put a large baking tray in. Remove your dough from the bowl and place it on a lightly floured surface and bash the air back out of it, then knead again for 1–2 minutes and shape it into a ball.

5. Flour the work surface and rolling pin and roll out the dough until it's about 28cm in diameter, then take the baking sheet out of the oven and slide the pizza base onto it. Spread the tomato sauce over the base and dot the mozzarella and basil leaves all over it, then scatter over the roasted vegetables season with a little salt and lots of freshly ground black pepper.

6. Place the baking tray in the oven and bake for 12 – 15 until the cheese is bubbling and the dough is golden, then remove and leave to stand for a couple of minutes before slicing and serving.

MARGHERITA PIZZA

SERVES 2 – 4
COSTS £1.50

Takes a bit of time but with a bit of practice...

Each portion contains

CALS	FAT	SALT
429	20g	1.2g
22%	25%	20%

of an adults' guideline daily amount

INGREDIENTS
200g can chopped tomatoes
1 clove garlic, crushed
1 tbls tomato puree
½ tsp caster sugar
1 tsp dried mixed herbs
1 ball mozzarella drained and torn into pieces
10 basil leaves
salt and pepper to taste

EQUIPMENT
Saucepan, measuring jug, wooden spoon,
sharp knife, baking tray, mixing bowl

1. Make a ball of dough according to the recipe on page 123.

2. While you're waiting for the dough you can make the sauce by placing the tomatoes into a small pan along with the garlic, tomato puree, sugar and mixed herbs. Stir and heat gently until the sauce thickens slightly, then set aside.

3. When the dough is ready, turn your oven on to gas mark 8 / 230°C and place a large baking tray into it. Remove your dough from the bowl and place it onto a lightly floured surface and bash the air back out of it, then knead again for 1–2 minutes and shape it into a ball.

4. Flour the work surface and rolling pin and roll out the dough until it's about 28cm in diameter, then take the baking sheet out of the oven and slide the pizza base onto it. Spread the tomato sauce over the base and dot the mozzarella and basil all over it, season with a little salt and lots of freshly ground black pepper.

5. Put the baking tray in the oven and bake for 12 – 15 until the cheese is bubbling and the dough is golden, then remove and leave to stand for a couple of minutes before slicing and serving.

LASAGNE

SERVES 2
COSTS £4

INGREDIENTS
lasagne sheets
1 small onion, chopped
300g minced lean beef
2 cloves garlic, finely chopped
1 tbls rosemary, chopped
1 tin chopped tomatoes
3 dried pasta sheets
150ml double cream
50g cheddar cheese, grated
2 tbls sunflower oil

EQUIPMENT
Sharp knife, chopping board, frying pan, saucepan, baking tray, peeler, rolling pin, mixing bowl, wooden spoon, whisk, blender, fork, sieve or colander, grater, hand blender, potato masher, pastry brush

1. Fry the mince in 1 tbls oil until brown. Sieve to get rid of the excess fat.

2. Put 1 tbls sunflower oil in a pan. Add the onion and garlic and cook for 2 – 3 minutes until soft but not coloured, then return the mince to the pan with a tin of tomatoes and the rosemary. Cook for 25 – 30 minutes on a medium heat.

3. Once the meat is cooked, place a small amount in the bottom of small casserole dish. Then add 50ml of cream and a sprinkle of cheese. Add a layer of lasagne sheets, repeat the process and finish with cream and cheese on top.

4. Cook in pre-heated oven gas mark 4 / 180°C for 30 minutes

RATATOUILLE

The food, not the film

SERVES 2
COSTS £2.50

INGREDIENTS
2 tomatoes, chopped
1 tbls olive oil
1 small onion, chopped
1 small red pepper, chopped
1 small yellow pepper, chopped
1 aubergine, diced
1 courgette, diced
1 tsp tomato puree
¼ tsp sugar
1 bay leaf
2 thyme sprigs
1 basil sprig
1 garlic glove
½ tbls chopped parsley

EQUIPMENT
Sharp knife, chopping board, frying pan, saucepan, wooden spoon

1. Heat the oil in a frying pan. Add the onions and cook over a low heat for 5 minutes, or until softened. Add the peppers and cook, stirring for 4 minutes. Remove from the pan and set aside.

2. Fry the aubergine until lightly browned all over and then remove from the pan. Fry the courgettes until browned and then return the onion, peppers and aubergine to the pan. Add the tomato puree, stir well and cook for 15 minutes. Add the tomato, sugar, bay leaf, thyme and basil, stir well, cover and cook for 15 minutes. Remove the bay leaf and thyme.

3. Mix together the garlic and parsley and add to the ratatouille at the last minute. Stir and serve.

MUSHROOM CARBONARA

SERVES 2
COSTS £3.25

INGREDIENTS
60g onion, chopped
1 clove garlic, chopped
12 button mushrooms, sliced
160g dried tagliatelle
a splash of white wine
3 tbls crème fraiche
30g parmesan, grated
2 tbls parsley, chopped
2 tbls chives, chopped
2 tbls sunflower oil
salt and pepper to taste

EQUIPMENT
Sharp knife, chopping board, frying pan, saucepan, grater, saucepan

1. Cook the tagliatelle in a pan, according to the packet instructions.

2. In a frying pan, add the oil and – when heated – the onion, garlic and mushrooms. Cook for 2 minutes.

3. When the onions, garlic and mushrooms are soft, add 3 tbls crème fraiche, parsley, chives and parmesan then add the cooked tagliatelle. Add salt and pepper if required. Warm through and serve.

Creamy Italian comfort food

SPINACH AND MUSHROOM FRITTATA

SERVES 4
COSTS £2

INGREDIENTS
6 eggs
3 tbls milk
3 tbls olive oil
300g button mushrooms, sliced
250g spinach, washed and drained
4 spring onions, finely sliced
1 clove garlic, crushed
2 tbls grated parmesan
2 tbls fresh basil, chopped
1 tbls fresh parsley, chopped
salt and pepper to taste

EQUIPMENT
1 non stick frying pan, whisk, wooden spoon, sharp knife

1. Crack the eggs into a bowl and add the milk, crushed garlic and half the parmesan and whisk well. Set aside and pre-heat your grill.

2. Heat a frying pan with the olive oil and fry the mushrooms for about 5 minutes, then add the spinach and continue to cook until most of the liquid has gone.

3. Add the eggs, basil and spring onions and season with salt and pepper. Mix well and cook over a medium heat for about 3 minutes.

4. Place the pan under the grill for about 1 minute or until the frittata has set, being careful not to burn the handle if plastic.

5. Sprinkle over the remaining parmesan and parsley and serve.

It's an omelette, but not as we know it

HILLI SQUID LINGUINE

SERVES 2
COSTS £5

INGREDIENTS
250g cooked spaghetti
medium squid, finely sliced
red chilli finely, diced
½ small diced onion
2 cloves crushed garlic
a handful basil leaves
4 chopped tomatoes
2 tbls capers
2 tbls chopped olives
2 tbls sweet chilli sauce
2 tbls sunflower oil
tsp chilli oil

EQUIPMENT
Sharp knife, chopping board, frying pan, saucepan, sieve

1. Cook the spaghetti in a saucepan as per the packet instructions, and set aside.

2. Add 2 tbls sunflower oil to hot pan – add the onion, garlic and chilli to the pan with the squid and cook for a couple of minutes.

3. Add the diced tomatoes, capers, olives, basil and cooked spaghetti. Cook for a further 2 minutes before adding sweet chilli sauce and chilli oil.

**Salad, spaghetti, seafood and spice –
this is one classy little number**

CLASSIC MEATBALLS IN TOMATO SAUCE

SERVES 2
COSTS £2.50

INGREDIENTS
500g minced beef
2 onions
2 cloves garlic, crushed
1 tbls dried mixed herbs
2 tbls fresh basil, chopped
2 cans chopped tomatoes
4 tbls olive oil
1 tsp sugar
salt and pepper

EQUIPMENT
1 large saucepan, frying pan, wooden spoon, sharp knife

1. Peel and finely chop 1 of the onions; heat a pan with 1 tbls olive oil and gently fry the onions until soft, then set aside.

2. Heat 1 tbls olive oil in a large pan and peel and finely dice the other onion, then fry along with 1 clove of garlic until starting to colour. Add the chopped tomatoes, sugar and basil, bring to a gentle simmer and leave for about 20 minutes, stirring from time to time. Add a little water if needed.

3. In a large bowl, mix the mince, cooked onion, 1 clove garlic, mixed herbs, 1 tsp salt, egg yolk and ½ tsp pepper. Squash with your hands until everything is combined well, then mould the mixture into balls a little bigger than golf balls and place in the fridge for 10 minutes.

4. Heat a frying pan with 2 tbls olive oil and fry the meatballs just enough to colour. Add them to the tomato sauce, cover and simmer for 10–15 minutes or until cooked through. Season the tomato sauce if needed and serve with pasta.

Let them soak in the sauce for a few hours for flawless flavour, and don't forget the garlic bread

Colourful, fresh, spicy and exotic, Mexican food relies heavily on corn and beans as the basis for many dishes. Corn is ground to make a dough used for tortillas, burritos and quesadilla; kidney beans pop up throughout Mexican cooking.

Its varied flavours stem from both sweet and spicy ingredients, including chilli powder, cumin, peppers and chipotle.

MEXIC

TACOS

A great little snack

SERVES 2
COSTS £3

INGREDIENTS
small onion, finely chopped
250g mince lean beef
¾ tsp cumin ground
¾ tsp chilli ground
½ tsp coriander ground
1 clove of garlic, chopped
2 tbls sunflower oil
1 baby gem lettuce
2 tbls low fat crème fraiche
a handful of crushed tortilla chips
1 red chilli, finely sliced
20g cheese, grated

EQUIPMENT
Sharp knife, chopping board, frying pan,
wooden spoon, grater

1. Heat 1 tbls of oil in frying pan; fry the mince until brown and drain.

2. Add the onion and garlic to the mince with the spices and cook for 5 minutes on a low heat.

3. When cooked, place in baby gem leaves. Sprinkle with crushed tortilla chips, crème fraiche and grated cheese.

Ava-dip

GUACAMOLE

SERVES 2 AS A DIP
COSTS £2

INGREDIENTS
1 mild chillies, finely chopped
½ bunch coriander, chopped
1 tomato, finely chopped
salt to taste
½ onion, finely chopped
1 tbls water
¼ lime, juice only
2 ripe avocados (scoop flesh out with a spoon)

EQUIPMENT
Sharp knife, chopping board, mixing bowl, fork, spoon

1. Mash the avocado with a fork and add the lime juice.

2. Combine the chillies, coriander, tomato, salt and onion with the avocado, adding water for your preferred thickness.

3. Once mixed, season to taste and serve.

TOMATO SALSA

SERVES 2 AS A DIP
COSTS £2

INGREDIENTS
250g tomatoes, deseeded and finely chopped
1 small red onion, finely diced
2 red or green mild chillies, finely diced
1 small bunch of coriander, chopped
½ lime, juice only
3 spring onions, finely chopped

EQUIPMENT
Mixing bowl, wooden spoon, chopping board

1. Combine all of the ingredients in a mixing bowl and mix together. Add salt and pepper if required and mix.

BEAN BURRITOS

SERVES 4 FOR LUNCH OR AS A SNACK
COSTS £3

INGREDIENTS
4 soft flour wraps
1 tbls sunflower oil
½ onion, chopped
1 clove garlic, crushed
1 small green pepper, thinly sliced
1 red chilli, deseeded and finely chopped
½ tsp ground cumin
200g can kidney beans, rinsed and drained
2 tomatoes, chopped
1 tbls sweet chilli sauce
1 tbls water
1 tbls fresh coriander, chopped
¼ iceberg lettuce, shredded
25g mature cheddar, grated
4 tbls yoghurt

EQUIPMENT
Sharp knife, saucepan, grater, mixing bowl

1. Heat the oil in a large frying pan; add the onion, garlic and green pepper and cook over a medium heat, stirring, for 3 minutes until they begin to soften. Add the red chilli and the ground cumin and stir for 1 minute.

2. Place the red kidney beans in a bowl and lightly crush with a fork, then add to the pan, together with the chopped tomatoes. Stir in the chilli sauce and the water and continue to cook gently for about 4 minutes, before stirring in the fresh coriander.

3. Serve the hot bean mixture, lettuce, cheese and yoghurt in bowls and warm the wraps gently under a grill or in the oven, so they're warm and soft. To assemble a burrito, put some lettuce in the middle of a wrap; spoon some bean mixture on top, add grated cheese and top with 1 tbls of yoghurt. Roll up and eat straight away. Continue to cook on a medium heat until set and golden brown on the bottom, then place the pan under a hot grill until set on top. (Make sure the handle is out of the grill if it is plastic.)

4. Turn out and cool before cutting into bite-sized pieces.

Burrito to eato

SPICY CHICKEN QUESADILLAS

SERVES 2
COSTS £2

INGREDIENTS
1 small chicken breast, diced
½ onion, sliced
1 red pepper, sliced
½ red-green chilli, sliced
½ tsp paprika
2 cloves garlic, crushed
half can of tomatoes
pack of tortillas (use 4)

EQUIPMENT
Sharp knife, chopping board, frying pan, baking tray, wooden spoon

1. Fry the onion, red pepper, chilli and garlic for 2 minutes until soft.

2. Add the chicken and paprika and cook for a further 2 – 3 minutes. Add the tomatoes and cook until chicken is cooked through – test by cutting a piece of chicken in half to make sure it's cooked.

3. Place a floured tortilla on a clean chopping board. Put a quarter of the mix in the middle of the tortilla and fold it over to create a half moon. Repeat with the remaining three tortillas. Place under a hot grill for 1–2 minutes each side or until crisp

Each portion contains		
CALS 479	**FAT** 26g	**SALT** 1.8g
25%	34%	29%
of an adults' guideline daily amount		

CHILLI CON CARNE

SERVES 1 AS A MAIN
COSTS £1

INGREDIENTS
150g lean minced beef
1 small onion, peeled and diced
½ clove garlic, crushed
2 tbls olive oil
½ tsp chilli powder
½ tsp ground cumin
½ tsp ground cinnamon
½ glass red wine (optional)
1 tin chopped tomatoes
1 tin kidney beans, drained
salt and pepper to taste

EQUIPMENT
Large pan, sharp knife, wooden spoon

1. Heat a pan with the olive oil; add the onions and beef and cook over a medium heat for about 5 minutes. Add the garlic, chilli powder, ground cumin and ground cinnamon and continue to cook for 1 more minute.

2. Add the red wine and cook until it has been absorbed, then add the can of tomatoes and simmer with a lid on for about 25 minutes, adding a little water if needed.

3. Add the kidney beans and stir, then continue to cook for a further 10 minutes.

4. Season to taste with a little salt and pepper and serve with boiled rice.

Like a big winter hug

FISH WITH LIME AND CHILLI SAUCE

SERVES 2
COSTS £3.50

INGREDIENTS
2 white fish fillets, cut into chunks
100g cornflour
3 tbls vegetable oil
2 garlic cloves, crushed
1 large red chillies, seeded and sliced
1 tsp soft light brown sugar
juice of 1 lime
grated rind of 1 lime

EQUIPMENT
Sharp knife, chopping board, frying pan, mixing bowl

1. Toss the fish in flour, shaking off any excess and cook in oil on both sides until crisp, using a frying pan.

2. Take the fish out of the frying pan and add the garlic and chillies, and stir fry for 1 – 2 minutes.

3. Add sugar, lime juice and rind and 2 – 3 tbls of water and bring to boil. Simmer gently for 1 – 2 minutes, and then spoon the mixture over the fish. Serve immediately with rice.

F-f-full of fishy flavour...

CHICKEN TORTILLA SOUP

Hearty, healthy and surprisingly filling for a soup

SERVES 4
COSTS £3.50

INGREDIENTS
4 corn tortillas, cut into strips
3 tbls olive oil
small onion, finely diced
2 cloves garlic, crushed
jalapeno chilli, deseeded and chopped
litre chicken stock
5 tomatoes, chopped
200g cooked chicken breast, shredded
or leftover chicken
ripe avocado, stone and skin removed and flesh diced
2 tbls fresh coriander, chopped

EQUIPMENT
Baking tray, saucepan, measuring jug, sharp knife

1. Place the tortilla strips on a baking tray and drizzle with
tbls of the olive oil, then place in a pre-heated oven at
gas mark 6 / 200°C for about 5 – 10 minutes or until crisp,
then remove and set aside.

2. Heat the remaining olive oil in a large pan and cook the
onion over a medium heat for about 5 minutes, then add
the garlic and chilli and continue to cook for a further 2
minutes. Now add the chicken stock and tomatoes and
bring to the boil, then simmer for about 15 minutes.

3. After 15 minutes, add the chicken and cook for another
5 minutes; season to taste with salt and pepper and stir in
the coriander.

4. To serve, divide the soup between 4 bowls, then add
some avocado and crispy tortilla

CARROT AND CORIANDER SOUP

SERVES 2 – 4
COSTS £1.50

INGREDIENTS
500g carrots, diced
2 cloves garlic, chopped
2 sticks celery, chopped
½ onion, chopped
1 leek, sliced
15g coriander ground
2 tbls olive oil
750ml vegetable stock

EQUIPMENT
Sharp knife, chopping board, saucepan, peeler,
hand blender

1. Add 2 tbls of oil to a pan – fry the onion, garlic and leek
until soft. Add the carrots and cook for 5 minutes. Add
the coriander powder and fry for a further 5 minutes on
a low heat.

2. Add the vegetable stock and cook until carrots are soft.

3. When the carrots are soft, blend with a hand blender
to a smooth consistency. If it's too thick add a little more
water or stock. Season with salt and pepper if required.

Sopa de la tortilla, as they say down Mexico way...

Plenty of those Mediterranean tastes are present again in saucy Spanish cooking. Olive oil, fresh fish, seafood and veg like onions, tomatoes and peppers are all there in numbers, as is the potato – a national favourite since swaggering Spanish explorers brought them back to Europe from the Americas in the 16th century. Pork is also popular across Spanish menus, either in its meaty form, or in chorizo or Serrano ham. Paprika, another popular spice, is what gives Spanish sausages their distinctive red colour...

SPAIN

PAELLA

You either love it or hate it

SERVES 4
COSTS £7

INGREDIENTS
1 skinless chicken breast, sliced
4 tbls sunflower oil
100g diced chorizo
1 medium onion, diced
1 crushed glove garlic
1 large red pepper, deseeded and sliced
pinch of saffron
500g mussels – discard any closed or broken shells
200g paella rice
100g frozen peas
¾ litre chicken stock

EQUIPMENT
Sharp knife, chopping board, frying pan, saucepan, mixing bowl, wooden spoon, sieve

1. Place mussels in a large saucepan with half of the chicken stock and saffron. Cook until mussels have opened for 2 – 3 minutes. Strain the pan through a fine sieve, keeping the juice, and set aside. Pick through the mussels removing them from the shell, and keep a couple of shells for decoration later. Discard the rest of shells.

2. Put 2 tbls sunflower oil in a frying pan and heat. Add the chorizo and chicken and cook until the chicken is cooked through. Take out of pan with a spoon and set aside. In same pan, add the onion, garlic and pepper and cook until softened. Add the chicken and chorizo to the pan, then mix rice into the mixture stirring until the rice is fully coated with the juices and mixture. Pour the mussel stock and remaining chicken stock into the pan. Cover with a lid or foil and cook on a medium to low heat for 10 – 15 minutes or until the rice is cooked (try not to stir too much during this process).

3. When the rice is nearly cooked, add the mussels and peas to the pan. Cover for 2 – 3 minutes until the peas are cooked. Serve.

PATATAS BRAVAS

SERVES 6 AS TAPAS
COSTS £1.60

INGREDIENTS
900g potatoes
5 tbls olive oil
1 small onion, peeled and finely diced
2 cloves garlic, crushed
1 can chopped tomatoes
1 tbls tomato puree
1 tbls smoked paprika
½ tsp chilli powder
2 tbls fresh parsley, chopped
salt and pepper to taste

EQUIPMENT
Sharp knife, baking tray, saucepan

1. Heat a pan with the 2 tbls olive oil and add the onions. Cook over a medium heat for about 5 minutes until soft, then add the garlic, tomatoes, tomato puree, paprika, chilli powder and a little salt, bring to the boil and simmer for about 10 minutes.

2. Peel the potatoes and cut into 2cm squares, then place into a baking tray and rub in the remaining olive oil. Season with a little salt and pepper and place into a pre-heated oven at gas mark 6 / 200°C for about 40 minutes, or until crisp outside and soft inside.

3. Remove the potatoes from the tray and place into a bowl, then pour the hot sauce over the top.

4. Serve with the parsley sprinkled over the top.

A tapas favourite

CHORIZO AND BROAD BEAN STEW

SERVES 2 AS MAIN / 8 AS TAPAS
COSTS £2.50

INGREDIENTS
2 tbls olive oil
1 tsp cumin seeds
2 cloves garlic, crushed
1 small onion, peeled and finely sliced
4 fresh chorizo sausages, skinned and diced
1 can chopped tomatoes
2 red peppers, cored and sliced
2 tsp smoked paprika
400g cooked broad beans
2 tbls fresh coriander, chopped
salt and pepper to taste

EQUIPMENT
Sharp knife, large pan, wooden spoon

1. Heat a pan with the olive oil and fry the onion for 5 minutes until soft; add the chorizo and garlic and continue to cook for 2 minutes.

2. Add the cumin seeds and cook for 30 seconds, then add the tomatoes, peppers, paprika and broad beans and simmer with a lid on for 15 minutes, adding a little water if needed.

3. Stir in the coriander and season to taste with salt and pepper.

4. Serve in bowls with boiled rice and crusty bread.

Great with the bravas

SPANISH FLATBREAD

It's skinny bread

SERVES 6 – 8
COSTS £3.50

INGREDIENTS
For the dough:
300g plain flour
1 sachet easy blend dried yeast
a pinch of sugar
½ tsp salt
2 tsp olive oil
250ml warm water

For the topping:
2 cloves garlic, crushed
4 large tomatoes, deseeded and finely sliced
2 courgettes, finely sliced
4 tbls olive oil
16 black olives
salt and pepper

EQUIPMENT
Large frying pan or wok, wooden spoon, mixing bowl, measuring jug, sharp knife

1. Put the flour, yeast, sugar and salt into a mixing bowl then add the water and mix until a dough forms. Tip out onto a work top and knead using your hands for about 5 minutes until smooth and elastic. Now return to the bowl and rub the 2 tsp of olive oil over the top, cover with cling film and leave in a warm place for about an hour.

2. After an hour, roll out the dough to about 2cm thick and place onto a baking tray lined with greaseproof paper.

3. Mix the crushed garlic with 2 tbls olive oil and spread over the base of the pizza, then arrange the remaining ingredients over the top. Season with salt and pepper and bake in a pre-heated oven gas mark 7 / 220°C for about 10 minutes or until crisp around the edges. Serve with a crisp green salad.

GAZPACHO

SERVES 2
COSTS £3

INGREDIENTS
400g ripe tomatoes, peeled and chopped
½ cucumber, peeled and chopped
2 red peppers, deseeded and chopped
1 red chilli, chopped
1 clove garlic, crushed
1 red onion, peeled and finely diced
1 tbls red wine vinegar
50 ml extra virgin olive oil
125g fresh white breadcrumbs
125ml cold water
salt and pepper to taste
1 tbls fresh parsley, chopped

EQUIPMENT
Sharp knife, food processor, mixing bowl, measuring jug

1. Place the tomatoes, cucumber, peppers, garlic, chilli, water, breadcrumbs and onions in a food processor and puree until almost smooth, leaving some texture. Stir in the olive oil and vinegar, mixing well, and put in the fridge for 2 hours.

2. Once the soup has been in the fridge for 2 hours and has chilled, stir in the chopped parsley, season with salt and freshly ground black pepper and serve.

SPANISH OMELETTE

SERVES 4 FOR LUNCH OR 10 AS TAPAS
COSTS £2.50

INGREDIENTS
3 large potatoes, peeled and sliced thinly into discs
50g butter
1 small onion, peeled and sliced
250g spinach, cooked and cooled
6 eggs
140ml double cream
salt and pepper to taste

EQUIPMENT
Sharp knife, non-stick pan, whisk, mixing bowl, measuring jug

1. Cook the potatoes in boiling water for about 5 minutes or until just tender, then carefully drain.

2. Heat the butter in a large non-stick frying pan and add the onions. Cook for about 5 minutes on a medium heat until softened, then add the potatoes and spinach and stir.

3. Whisk the eggs and cream in a bowl and season with salt and pepper, then add the egg mixture to the pan and stir to combine. Continue to cook on a medium heat until set and golden brown on the bottom, then place the pan under a hot grill until set on top (make sure the handle is out of the grill if it is plastic).

4. Turn out and leave to cool before cutting into bite-sized pieces.

We cut ours up into strips – because we can

GARLIC SOUP

Garlic soup, garlic crouton and a garlicky egg. One for garlic lovers everywhere...

SERVES 4
COSTS £1.50

INGREDIENTS
4 slices of bread from a good loaf
6 cloves garlic, lightly crushed
6 tbls olive oil
1 tsp smoked paprika
1 tsp hot paprika
½ tsp ground cumin
1 ¼ litres chicken stock
4 very fresh eggs
salt and pepper

EQUIPMENT
Sharp knife, 4 ovenproof soup bowls, saucepan, measuring jug

1. Place the bread under a medium grill and toast until golden on both sides – remove and rub each piece on one side with a clove of garlic. Drizzle over half the olive oil and place in 4 ovenproof soup bowls, then set aside.

2. Heat the remaining olive oil in a pan and add the garlic. Fry over a medium heat until the garlic is golden, then stir in the smoked and hot paprika and the ground cumin; add the chicken stock and simmer for 5 minutes.

3. Season to taste with salt and pepper, then pour over the bread into the soup bowls. Crack one egg into each and place into a pre-heated oven at gas mark 6 / 200°C until the egg white has set, but the yolk is still runny, and serve straight away.

CHICKEN AND CHORIZO EMPANADAS

MAKES 6 – 8 PASTIES
COSTS £3.50

INGREDIENTS
For the pastry:
175g plain flour
60g butter
1 egg
50ml warm water

For the filling:
1 large chicken fillet, thinly sliced
3 boiled eggs, quartered
100g chorizo, diced
1 small onion, thinly sliced
½ large red pepper, sliced
50ml white wine
2 tbls chopped coriander
2 tbls sunflower oil

EQUIPMENT
Sharp knife, chopping board, frying pan, saucepan, baking tray, rolling pin, mixing bowl, wooden spoon, pastry brush

1. Put 2 tbls sunflower oil in a pan. Add the onion, red pepper and chorizo, and cook for 2 minutes, before adding the chicken and cooking for another 2 to 3 minutes. Add the white wine until evaporated, then add the chopped coriander. When the chicken's cooked, place it on a tray and leave to cool.

2. Melt the butter with the water, then add to the flour and combine using a wooden spoon to make a warm dough.

3. While the dough is still warm, divide into 10 small balls and roll out to 10cm circles. Put the chilled chicken and chorizo mix into the middle of the pastry, with 2 pieces of boiled egg on top of the chicken mix. Fold over pastry to the centre to create a half moon shape.

4. Pre-heat the oven to gas mark 4 / 180°C and place on baking tray, cooking for 15 to 20 minutes until golden.

They're pasties, but made the Spanish way!

Soup, rice, curry, fish – all play their part in our dip into the aromatic world of Thai food. Thai – with its Chinese and Indian influences – is the perfect comfort food... Fresh, rich, spicy and warm, with all those deep fragrant smells to fill the dining room.

TON

You could almost be there

...UM SOUP

SERVES 2
COSTS £2

INGREDIENTS
600ml vegetable stock
100ml water
3 lemongrass sticks, lightly crushed
5cm piece of ginger, peeled and sliced
4 tomatoes, deseeded and chopped
3 kaffir lime leaves
juice from 1 lime
35ml tamarind water (soak tamarind in water and sieve)
2 red chillies, finely diced
35ml fish sauce
35g brown sugar
1 red pepper, deseeded and sliced
100g mixed mushrooms, sliced
1 small bunch coriander leaves

EQUIPMENT
2 large saucepans, measuring jug, wooden spoon,
sharp knife

1. Add the stock, water, lemongrass, ginger, tomatoes,
lime juice, lime leaves, tamarind water and red chillies to
a large pan and bring to the boil. Reduce the heat and
simmer for 15 minutes.

2. Now add most of the fish sauce and sugar saving a little
back to add later if needed, mix and cook for 2 minutes
more, and then taste. Some stocks are saltier than others
so you can add more fish sauce and sugar if needed – it
should taste a mixture of hot, sweet, sour and salty.

3. Remove the ginger and lemongrass and add the peppers
and mushrooms and cook for about 10 minutes until the
peppers have softened.

4. Stir in the coriander and divide between 2 bowls.

Each portion contains		
CALS 224	**FAT** 5g	**SALT** 3.6g
12%	7%	60%

of an adults' guideline daily amount

THAI GREEN CHICKEN SALAD

One for the summer

SERVES 2 FOR LUNCH
COSTS £3.25

INGREDIENTS
2 chicken breasts, cooked and cooled
¼ large red cabbage, shredded
1 red onion, peeled and finely sliced
1 cucumber, cored and sliced
2 carrots, peeled and sliced into matchsticks
100g mangetout
3 tbls olive oil
200ml low fat coconut milk
3 tbls Thai green curry paste
1 tbls lemon juice
10 fresh mint leaves, shredded
1 large handful fresh coriander, chopped
salt and pepper to taste

EQUIPMENT
Large mixing bowl, small mixing bowl, sharp knife

1. Shred the chicken breasts and add to a bowl along
with the red cabbage, red onion, cucumber, carrots and
mangetout, then set aside.

2. In a small mixing bowl, whisk together the Thai green
curry paste and coconut milk, then whisk in the olive oil
and lemon juice.

3. Add the coconut milk dressing and mint leaves to the
salad and mix well. Season with salt and pepper to taste
and serve in small bowls.

PAD THAI

MAKES 2 PORTIONS
COSTS £4

INGREDIENTS
125g thick rice stick noodles
1 tbls sunflower oil
1 garlic clove, chopped
1 fresh red chilli, seeded and chopped
1 chicken fillet
100g cooked prawns
2 spring onions, finely chopped
1 tbls fish sauce
2 tbls chives
juice of 1 lime
1 tsp soft light brown sugar
1 egg, beaten
a handful of beansprouts
2 tbls chopped coriander
50g chopped unsalted peanuts, plus extra to serve

EQUIPMENT
Sharp knife, chopping board, frying pan/wok,
mixing bowl

1. Soak the noodles in warm water for 10 minutes, drain
and set aside.

2. Heat the oil in a wok and stir fry the garlic, chillies and
chicken for 2 – 3 minutes. Add the prawns and stir fry for
another 2 – 3 minutes.

3. Add the chives and noodles, then cover and cook for
1 – 2 minutes. Finish by adding the fish sauce, lime juice,
sugar and egg, stirring throughout and tossing constantly
to mix the egg.

4. Finally, stir in the beansprouts, coriander and peanuts
and serve with extra chopped peanuts.

An eastern favourite with an Irish twist

PORK SATAY WITH PEANUT SAUCE

SERVES 2 AS A STARTER
COSTS £2.50

INGREDIENTS
For the pork skewers:
200g pork tenderloin
1 shallot, peeled and chopped
1 clove garlic, peeled and chopped
¼ tsp ground cumin
¼ tsp ground turmeric
½ tsp ground coriander
½ small green chilli
2 tbls fish sauce
½ tbls dark soy sauce
1 tbls honey
65ml low fat coconut milk

For the peanut sauce:
150g unsalted peanuts
80ml water
2 cloves garlic crushed
½ tsp dark soy sauce
2 tsp sesame oil
2 tbls brown sugar
2 tbls fish sauce
½ tsp lime juice
½ tsp cayenne pepper
80ml low fat coconut milk
juice from ½ lime

EQUIPMENT
Food processor, mixing bowl, baking tray, sharp knife,
4 wooden skewers

How to make the pork skewers:
1. Soak the wooden skewers in cold water for 30 minutes
to stop them from burning when you cook the pork.

2. Slice the pork into long strips about half an inch wide
and put in a bowl.

3. To marinate the pork, place the shallot, garlic, cumin,
turmeric, coriander, green chilli, fish sauce, lime juice, soy,
coconut milk and honey in a small food processor and blitz
into a paste, then add to the bowl with the pork and add
the coconut milk and mix well. Leave to marinate for at
least 30 minutes (the longer the better)

4. While the pork is marinating place all of the ingredients
for the peanut sauce in a food processor and blend until
smooth, adding a little more water if you prefer your sauce
to be runnier.

5. When the pork has marinated, skewer the meat onto
the sticks weaving lengthways along the skewers and
place on a baking tray. With the grill set to medium, cook
the satay for about 6 – 8 minutes turning a few times and
making sure not to burn them.

6. When ready, serve with peanut sauce and crisp lettuce
leaves like little gems.

Ultimate takeaway fodder.
Easy to cook, easy to eat.

NASI GORENG

SERVES 2
COSTS £2

INGREDIENTS
2 eggs, beaten
2 red chillies, seeded and shredded
1 onion, finely sliced
1 garlic clove, finely chopped
1 carrot, grated
150g sliced chestnut mushrooms
200g uncooked basmati rice
2 tsp soft brown sugar
1 tbls soy sauce
2 tbls chilli sauce
¼ cucumber, finely sliced
a drizzle of sesame oil

EQUIPMENT
Sharp knife, chopping board, frying pan, saucepan, mixing bowl, wooden spoon, whisk, grater, sieve, peeler

1. Cook the rice as per the packet instructions.

2. Fry the eggs into an omelette and slice into shreds once cooked. Set aside.

3. Heat the oil in a pan on medium heat. Add the onion, chilli, garlic, carrot and mushrooms and fry for 4 minutes. Add the cooked rice.

4. Mix together the sugar, soy sauce and chilli sauce and then add to the rice mix.

5. Divide into two bowls. Add the sliced cucumber, shredded omelette and drizzle with sesame oil and serve.

OK, so we know it's not strictly Thai but it's well tasty. Save some for breakfast.

BEEF RANDANG

This is what happens when you piss cows off

SERVES 4
COSTS £5

INGREDIENTS
500g braising steak
1 can coconut milk
150ml water
1 lime leaf
1 small piece of cinnamon
4 cardamom pods, lightly crushed
salt and pepper

Spice mix:
1 piece of lemon grass (white only)
1 small onion
6 red chillis
4 cloves garlic
5cm piece of ginger
½ tsp of ground cloves
½ tsp of ground turmeric
1 tsp ground coriander
1 tsp ground cumin

EQUIPMENT
Blender, sauce pan, frying pan, sieve, wooden spoon

1. Firstly, place the steak in a saucepan, cover with water, bring to the boil and simmer for 30 minutes.

2. Put all of the spice ingredients in a blender and blend to form a paste.

3. Heat 3 tbls of oil in a frying pan, add the spice mix and fry on a low heat until fragrant and a dark colour. Then add the meat and coat well.

4. Once the meat is well coated, add the coconut milk and water and whole spices. Bring to the boil and simmer for one to one and half hours, or until the meat is tender.

5. When the curry is ready, it will become darker and drier – at this point it is ready to serve. Be careful not to burn the bottom of the pan. Serve with rice.

THAI GREEN CHICKEN CURRY

SERVES 2
COSTS £3, INCLUDING RICE

A great curry for people who don't like curries

INGREDIENTS

For the curry paste:
2 lemongrass sticks with the outer leaves removed and the inside finely chopped
2 green chillies, chopped
2 small cloves garlic, peeled and chopped
2.5cm piece of ginger, peeled and chopped
1 shallot, peeled and chopped
2 tbls fresh coriander, chopped (stalks are fine to use)
½ tsp ground cumin
zest from ½ lime
1 tbls fish sauce
¼ tsp ground black pepper

For the curry:
350g diced chicken thighs, skinned and boned
2 tbls sunflower oil
100g chestnut mushrooms, quartered
200ml low fat coconut milk
200ml chicken stock – Knorr is fine
4 kaffir lime leaves
1 tbls fish sauce
½ tbls green peppercorns in brine (drained)
2 tbls green curry paste from above
a small bunch of basil and coriander, chopped

Each portion contains		
CALS 744	**FAT** 54g	**SALT** 3g
38%	72%	49%
of an adults' guideline daily amount		

EQUIPMENT
Food processor, large pan, wooden spoon, sharp knife, measuring jug

Making the paste
Place all of the ingredients for the paste in a food processor and whizz to a thick paste, pushing the mixture down from time to time with a spoon. Transfer to an airtight container (otherwise it'll taint everything in the fridge) and refrigerate.

Making the curry
1. Heat the oil in a large pan and add the chicken – fry until golden and remove from the pan, then add the mushrooms and do the same.

2. Now add the coconut milk and stock to the pan, then add the lime leaves and 2 large tbls of the paste, the fish sauce, peppercorns and half of the herbs. Mix well and bring to the boil, then simmer for 8 – 10 minutes.

3. Add the chicken, mushrooms and ½ tbls more of the curry paste, simmer for about 5 minutes until the chicken is cooked and add the rest of the herbs. Serve with Thai fragrant rice.

THAI FISHCAKES

SERVES 4
COST £3

INGREDIENTS
500g white fish
1 red chilli, diced
1 tsp fish sauce
2 tbls curry paste (see Penang chicken curry, page 111)
50g green beans, sliced
3 spring onions, finely sliced
1 egg white
2 heaped tbls coriander
2 tbls vegetable oil

Each portion contains		
CALS 194	**FAT** 11g	**SALT** 1.8g
10%	45%	29%
of an adults' guideline daily amount		

EQUIPMENT
Food processor, bowl, sharp knife, frying pan

1. Combine all of the ingredients – except the green beans and spring onions – in the food processor. Blend into a paste.

2. Transfer into a bowl and then add green beans and spring onions to the mixture.

3. Make the mixture into six balls and flatten.

4. Heat a pan with the oil and fry the cakes for 3 to 5 minutes or until browned.

5. Serve with dipping sauce (see page 123) and a salad garnish.

Something fishy going on

THAI MUSSELS

SERVES 2
COSTS £3

INGREDIENTS
500g mussels
1 tbls green curry paste
100ml coconut milk
50ml white wine
1 chilli, finely shredded
2 cloves garlic, finely sliced
2.5cm piece of ginger, peeled and finely sliced
3 tbls fresh coriander, chopped
1 tbls sunflower oil

EQUIPMENT
Sharp knife, chopping board, saucepan

1. Place 1 tbls of sunflower oil in a saucepan. Fry the curry paste and garlic for 1 minute to release the flavours, and add the mussels.

2. Put the white wine and coconut milk into a pan – place a lid on top of mussels on a high heat for 3 – 4 minutes or until the mussels have opened.

3. When the mussels are cooked, add finely sliced chilli, ginger and coriander.

Easier than you think – have a go

PENANG CHICKEN CURRY

SERVES 4 – 6
COSTS £6

INGREDIENTS
For the paste:
8 large red chillies, deseeded and chopped
1 large onion, chopped
6 gloves garlic, chopped
1 tsp ground coriander
1 tsp ground cumin
2 stems lemon grass – white part only, roughly chopped
2.5cm fresh ginger, chopped
2 tbls roasted peanuts

For the curry:
100g creamed coconut
600g boneless skinless chicken thigh
400ml low fat coconut milk
90g crunchy peanut butter
juice of 2 limes
2½ tbls fish sauce
4 tbls light brown sugar
basil to garnish

EQUIPMENT
Sharp knife, chopping board, frying pan, saucepan, baking tray, peeler, rolling pin, mixing bowl, wooden spoon, whisk, blender, fork, sieve or colander, skewer, grater, hand blender, potato masher, pastry brush

1. Put the ingredients for the paste in a food processor and pulse to a smooth paste, adding water if needed.

2. Stir 8 tbls of the paste with the creamed coconut and cook for 5–10 minutes on a medium heat. Stir often, making sure it doesn't stick to the pan.

3. Add the chicken, coconut milk and peanut butter to the mixture and remaining coconut cream. Reduce the heat and simmer for 20 minutes, stirring every few minutes. Add water if needed.

4. Stir in the lime juice, fish sauce and sugar and cook for a further 5 minutes. Serve in a bowl and garnish with basil.

It's not quite Thai, but it's still too good to resist!

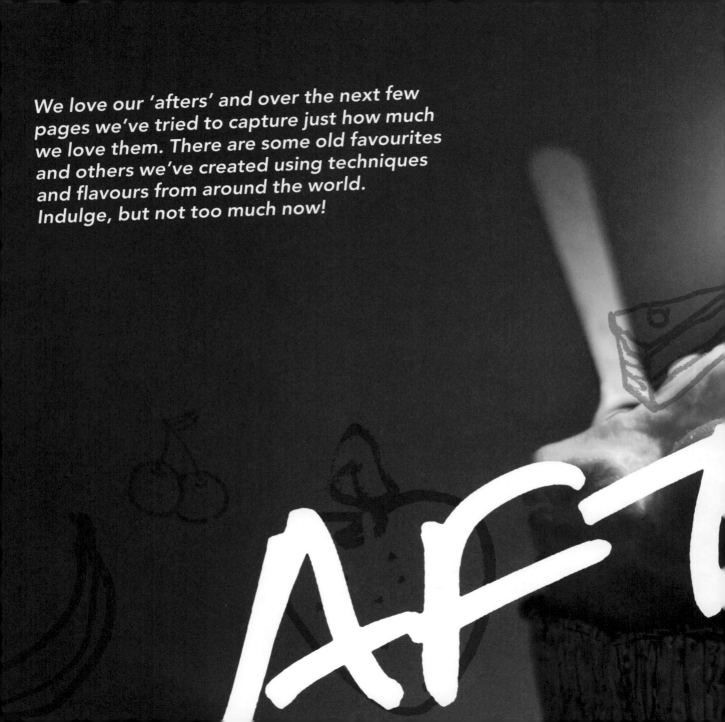

We love our 'afters' and over the next few pages we've tried to capture just how much we love them. There are some old favourites and others we've created using techniques and flavours from around the world. Indulge, but not too much now!

BANANA SPLIT

SERVES 2
COSTS £3.25

INGREDIENTS
2 large bananas, peeled and sliced in half lengthways
20g caster sugar
4 strawberries
10 raspberries
10g flaked almonds, crushed
4 scoops of vanilla ice cream
2 tbls condensed caramel

EQUIPMENT
Sharp knife, chopping board, mixing bowl

1. Place the bananas in bowl and sprinkle sugar over them. Put them under grill until golden brown.

2. Place the bananas in the middle of plate and arrange strawberries and raspberries around them. Scoop ice cream on top of the bananas and sprinkle the almonds over. Drizzle caramel over bananas.

La-la-la, la-la-la-laaaa!
One banana, two banana...

APPLE, PEAR AND CHILLI SAMOSAS

SERVES 2
COSTS £2

INGREDIENTS
1 apple – we use golden delicious
– cored and diced into 1cm squares
1 pear – we use conference
– cored and diced into 1 cm squares
20g caster sugar
60g butter
½ long red chilli, deseeded and finely diced
juice from ½ lemon
2 sheets filo pastry

EQUIPMENT
Small knife, pastry brush, sauce pan, frying-pan, wooden spoon, baking tray

1. Place half of the butter and half of the sugar in the frying pan and melt over a medium heat. When the butter's melted, add the diced apple and pear with the finely diced chilli. Cook for two minutes then add the lemon juice. Cook for two more minutes or until the fruit is soft. Place on baking tray and chill.

2. Cut the filo in half lengthways. If you're using fresh filo, you can freeze the rest of it. Melt the remaining butter and take one piece of filo pastry and brush with the melted butter. Place a quarter of the filling at one end of the strip, leaving a 2cm border. Take the right corner and fold diagonally to the left, enclosing the filling and forming a triangle. Fold again along the crease and continue to do this until you reach the end. Brush with a little more butter and place on a baking tray lined with greaseproof paper, then repeat the process with the rest of the mixture.

3. When all of the samosas are made, cook in a pre-heated oven at gas mark 4 / 180°C for 15 – 20 minutes, checking after 10 minutes. Remove from the oven and serve.

Bet you like them

115

FRUIT SALAD

SERVES 4
COSTS £3.30

INGREDIENTS
2 oranges
2 ripe pears
2 royal gala apples
50g grapes black seedless
50g grapes green seedless
1 star fruit
a tub of low fat crème fraiche

For the syrup:
200g caster sugar
100ml water
2 pieces peeled lemon rind
2 pieces peeled lime rind

EQUIPMENT
Sharp knife, chopping board, saucepan, peeler,
mixing bowl

1. To make the syrup, combine all of the syrup ingredients
and bring to boil. Take off the heat and leave to cool.

2. Segment the oranges in a bowl, slice the apples and
pears, halve the grapes and slice the star fruit (any fruit
can be used – you choose).

3. When the syrup is cool, pour over the fruit and leave to
chill in the fridge for 1 hour.

4. Serve in a wine glass with a dollop of crème fraiche.

*It's fruit that you make into
a salad. Revolutionary...*

NEW YORK CHEESECAKE

SERVES 12
COSTS £6

INGREDIENTS
16 digestive biscuits
150g melted butter
220g caster sugar
800g cream cheese
200g sour cream
2 eggs
2 egg yolk
½ tsp vanilla extract

EQUIPMENT
30cm loose-bottomed cake tin, saucepan, baking tray,
rolling pin, mixing bowl, wooden spoon, whisk

1. Crush the biscuits by hand or with a rolling pin. Pour the
melted butter over them and mix together, before putting
them in the bottom of cake tin to make a thin layer.

2. Add sugar and cream cheese to a bowl and lightly
whisk. Add sour cream, the eggs, egg yolks and vanilla
extract and continue to whisk into a smooth mixture.

3. Pour the mixture over the biscuit base and cook in a
pre-heated oven at gas mark 2 / 150°C for 1 hour or until
firm to touch.

Lovely

BANOFFEE PIE

SERVES 6 – 8
COSTS £5

INGREDIENTS
150g plain flour
115g diced cold butter
50g caster sugar
3 large bananas
350ml double cream
4 tsp grated chocolate eg Dairy Milk
2 tins condensed milk (caramel)

EQUIPMENT
Sharp knife, chopping board, frying pan, saucepan, baking tray, peeler, rolling pin, mixing bowl, wooden spoon, whisk, blender, fork, sieve or colander, skewer, grater, hand blender, potato masher, pastry brush

1. Firstly, make the pastry by combining the plain flour, butter and sugar in a food processor or by hand and mix to a soft, pliable dough.

2. Roll the pastry out, place it in a quiche tin and blind bake (blind baking means baking the pastry crust without the filling. Line the pastry with tin foil or baking paper, and fill with dried peas, lentils, beans – or ceramic 'baking beans', so it keeps its shape when cooking.) for 25 – 30 minutes in a pre-heated oven at gas mark 4 / 180°C.

3. When cooked and cooled, put the caramel into the pastry base. Cover with sliced banana, then pile the whipped cream on top, finishing with the grated chocolate.

A banoffee to scoffy

GREEN TEA PANNA COTTA

SERVES 6
COSTS £3

INGREDIENTS
150ml milk
500ml double cream
3 green tea teabags
50g caster sugar
3 leaves bronze leaf gelatine
½ tsp vanilla extract

EQUIPMENT
Saucepan, whisk, mixing bowl, measuring jug

1. Place the gelatine in a bowl and cover with cold water, then set aside. Put the teabags and milk – along with 250ml of double cream – in a saucepan and bring slowly to the boil, then simmer for 5 minutes. After 5 minutes, turn off the heat and remove the tea bags, squeezing out any liquid in them.

2. Now, using your hands, take the gelatine out of the water and gently squeeze out any excess liquid, then add to the pan and whisk until it has dissolved. Allow the mixture to cool down as quickly as you can (we place the pan into a sink of cold water, making sure no water gets into the pan).

3. While the mixture is cooling, place the remaining cream in a bowl along with the vanilla extract and whip until you can lift the whisk out and it leaves a ribbon effect in the cream – this is known as 'soft peaks'.

5. Fold the whipped cream into the milk and cream mixture until well combined, and divide between 6 small moulds. Put in the fridge until it's set – this should take about 2 hours.

6. To serve, dip the bottom of the mould in boiling water for a couple of seconds and turn upside down onto a plate.

China meets Italy

CHOCOLATE AND CARDAMOM MOUSSE

Sugar and spice and all things nice!

SERVES 6
COSTS £2

INGREDIENTS
200g plain chocolate
4 eggs, separated
25g light muscovado sugar
4 cardamom pods, split and seeds crushed

EQUIPMENT
Whisk, 3 mixing bowls, spatula, sauce pan

1. Put the chocolate and cardamom into a bowl and place over a pan of simmering water, then gently melt.

2. Separate the eggs, with the yolks in one bowl and the whites into another. Add the sugar to the yolks and whisk until it becomes light and fluffy. Whisk the egg whites until stiff peaks form – you should be able to lift out the whisk and the egg white will stay in a point.

3. When the chocolate has melted, add to the egg yolk mixture, then fold the egg whites in – a little at a time – until all the whites have been mixed in. Try not to over mix at this point or you will lose the air out of the mousse.

4. Once you've combined all the ingredients, pour into one large bowl or individual moulds and place into the fridge to chill for at least 1 hour, then serve.

APPLE CRUMBLE

To make your tum-bley rumble

SERVES 2
COSTS £3

INGREDIENTS
60g butter
120g sugar (caster or demerara)
120g flour
300g bramley apple
2 tbls water

EQUIPMENT
Sharp knife, chopping board, saucepan, baking tray, peeler, mixing bowl, wooden spoon, casserole dish

1. To make the crumble combine all of the flour and butter together then mix in 60g of the sugar until it's a breadcrumb consistency.

2. Peel and chop the bramley apple. Place in pan with 60g of the sugar and 2 tbls water. Put on a high heat with the lid on to start with, then turn down heat until apple is soft but not a puree.

3. Place the apple in small casserole dish and sprinkle over the crumble.

4. Bake in a pre-heated oven at gas mark 4 / 180°C for 30 minutes.

STOCKS + SAUCES

Stocks form the basis for stacks of our dishes – wherever in the world they're from – from soups to sauces. These are two classic stock recipes – dead easy to master, you can freeze them for up to six months, pulling them out to defrost as and when you need them....

CHICKEN STOCK

INGREDIENTS
4 raw chicken carcasses
1 whole head of garlic, cut in half
5 sticks of celery, chopped
2 leeks, chopped
2 onions, chopped
2 carrots, chopped
3 bay leaves
2 sprigs of rosemary
5 sprigs of thyme
1 small bunch of parsley
5 black peppercorns
4 litres cold water

EQUIPMENT
A stock pot or very large saucepan, sharp knife, ladle

1. Put the chicken carcasses in the stockpot and cover with cold water, bring slowly to the boil, and simmer uncovered for 1 hour. Make sure you skim off the frothy scum that comes to the surface.

2. After an hour, add all of the other ingredients and simmer for a further 2 hours – continue to skim any more scum that froths on top, but never stir the stock or it will be greasy when finished.

3. After 2 hours, strain the stock and discard the bones and vegetables. Return to the heat and reduce to 3 litres, then allow to cool and remove the hard fat that has settled on top. You can now divide into smaller portions and keep in the fridge for 4 days or the freezer for 3 – 4 months until needed.

VEGETABLE STOCK

INGREDIENTS
4 carrots, chopped
3 large onions, peeled and chopped
4 sticks celery, chopped
½ bulb fennel, chopped
stalk from a head of broccoli
4 tomatoes, cut in half
10 black peppercorns
2 bay leaves
3 sprigs of thyme
1 small bunch parsley
3 litres cold water

EQUIPMENT
A stock pot or very large saucepan, a sharp knife, ladle

1. Put all of the ingredients in a large pan and bring to the boil, then reduce the heat and simmer uncovered for 40 minutes.

2. After 40 minutes, strain out all of the vegetables, then return to the heat and reduce the stock by boiling until you have approximately 2 litres. Allow to cool and use as needed or freeze in smaller portions.

SWEET CHILLI DIPPING SAUCE

INGREDIENTS
500ml white wine vinegar
500g caster sugar
5cm piece ginger, peeled and finely diced
4 red chillies, deseeded and finely diced
10cm piece of cucumber, finely diced

1. Put the vinegar and sugar in a pan and bring to a boil; reduce by a third and take off and cool when ready.

2. Add the chilli, ginger and cucumber and serve.

SALT + PEPPER SPICE MIX

INGREDIENTS
1 tbls chilli
1 tbls paprika
¼ tsp turmeric
½ tsp curry powder
½ ground fenugreek
2 tbls szechuan peppercorns
1 tbls sugar

EQUIPMENT
Blender, pestle and mortar

Place all of the ingredients in a pestle and mortar and grind or blend to a fine powder.

BBQ SAUCE

INGREDIENTS
120g onion, finely chopped
3 cloves garlic, crushed
1 red chilli, finely chopped
1 tsp fennel seeds
50ml dark soy sauce
300ml tomato ketchup
1 tsp fresh ginger grated

EQUIPMENT
Sharp knife, wooden spoon, large saucepan, grater, measuring jug

1. Put all of the ingredients in a food processor and blend, then use as directed in your recipe.

DOUGH

INGREDIENTS
175g strong white bread flour
1 tsp salt
1 tsp fast action dried yeast
1 tbls olive oil
120ml tepid water

EQUIPMENT
Measuring jug, wooden spoon, mixing bowl

1. Put the flour in a large mixing bowl and add the yeast and 1 tsp of salt, then add the olive oil and water. Mix using a spoon at first and then your hands, until a ball of dough has formed.

2. Tip the dough out onto your worktop and knead for about 4–5 minutes, adding a little flour if the dough is too sticky to handle. Put the dough back into the mixing bowl and cover with cling film – leave in a warm place for 1 hour until it has doubled in size.

MEET THE TEAM

Alex adores the good old bangers and mash (pg 26)
Fiona's favourite is the shepherd's pie (pg 21)
Lucy loves Thai green chicken curry (pg 108)
Mike's mad for our New York cheesecake (pg 116)
Richie's ravin' about the mussels (pg 111)
Robbie's relishing a pork vindaloo (pg 65)
Tony's top tip is his Two Tin Curry Dinner (pgs 6–7).

PARTNERS

This book was created with the support of two important programmes which have been set up to improve young peoples' education in Liverpool, and change and improve the nutritional culture of takeaway outlets in Liverpool.

A bit about their work...

EXTENDED SCHOOLS

Extended Schools is a national programme to take forward the Government's aspirations for every school (secondary, primary and special) to provide their pupils, parents/carers and local families with access to a core of extended services. Extended services are activities mainly delivered before and after school, and during lunch breaks, weekends and holidays.

The aim of the programme is to support the raising achievement agenda by contributing to a child's ability to achieve his or her full potential. It encourages parents and carers of underachieving, disengaged and vulnerable students to participate in their children's education, through the development of creative and innovative activities that capture the interest of children and young people.

Liverpool Extended Schools works at a strategic level in the local authority and with clusters of schools, helping them provide access to a range of activities and services beyond the school day. These activities help meet the needs of children, their families and communities, according to local need.

EATRIGHT

In 2005/6 Liverpool City Council Trading Standards Department began a healthy eating project to improve the health of the citizens of Liverpool. The project concentrated on one of the most unregulated sectors of the food retail industry – takeaway establishments. In the UK there is no legal provision for such businesses to state what's in the food they supply, or to show the nutritional content of that food. The nutritional balance in takeaway outlets is generally poor and exacerbated by the demands of 'fast food' – deep fat frying and other unhealthy cooking methods – which significantly increase fat and calorie content.

Over 300 takeaway meals were purchased and analysed for salt, fat and calorific content. One Chinese meal, beef green pepper and black bean sauce with fried rice, was found to contain 27.6g of salt – nearly five times the 6g RDA for an adult. Pizzas were found to contain both large amounts of fat and calories. The results show an urgent need to change the food consumed from takeaway establishments.

As a result, Liverpool Primary Care Trust is funding the Eatright Liverpool project. Liverpool Trading Standards is working in partnership with Liverpool John Moores University to improve the nutritional content of takeaway and restaurant food without compromising the taste, texture, cost and customer appeal.

ACKNOWLEDGEMENTS

A few words from Robbie...

Without everyone mentioned here this book would never have happened:

Tony: This year has been a big year for us and you and this book is our best yet. Once again you've stood up and made the difference – Can Cook owes you a lot.

Richie: You have a flair for it all and have become a real asset to us – like Tony, you have made a difference – thanks.

Lucy: You and I know how hard you have worked to manage all that we have. It's coming together – thank you.

Fiona: What can I say? You make everything gel. I love working with you.

Mike: For creating that takeaway feel. It's dark and funky – just what we wanted – you've got a talent.

Alex: The pictures are that good they lift off the page. It was great to watch you work and bring it all to life – cheers.

And a big thank you to

Si and Charlotte (for letting us in...); Susan Roberts, Angie Gilbert, Julie Davies, Collette O'Brien, Colin Wayland, Rachel Long, Julie Curren, Brian Jones, Irene Mills, Louise Wills, Deirdre and Emma (for the props), and Dave from Pizza Hut in Speke (for the pizza boxes).

Thank you to our funders

Liverpool Extended Schools, Liverpool Trading Standards (Eatright) and Taste for Health.

INDEX